JOHN NICHOLSON

John is a writer, performer and dir
the award-winning Peepolykus, with whom he has created twelve
productions that have toured the company worldwide and into the West
End with *The Hound of the Baskervilles* (which has also been licensed
over 200 times worldwide). It's published by Nick Hern Books
alongside four of John's other adaptations: *The Massive Tragedy of
Madame Bovary*, *Dracula: The Bloody Truth*, *The Three Musketeers*
and *Treasure Island*. For BBC Radio 4, John has written two afternoon
plays, two series of *A Trespasser's Guide to the Classics* and a series of
short stories with Rik Mayall. Writing/performing credits for TV
include BBC3, BBC2, Paramount and ITV. Writing/directing
commissions for theatre include Aardman, Liverpool Everyman and
Playhouse, Bristol Old Vic, Lyric Hammersmith, Leeds Playhouse,
Traverse Edinburgh, Jermyn Street Theatre, Barbican Plymouth,
Sydney Opera House, Pickled Image, National Youth Theatre,
BritishYMT, LIPA, Bath Theatre Royal, Pentabus, London Old Vic,
Royal National Theatre, Spymonkey, Paul Merton, Nina Conti, Neal
Street Productions and theatre company Le Navet Bete. He has
recently completed a three-hander adaptation of *The Time Machine*.
More details at johnnicholsoncomedytheatredirector.com

LE NAVET BETE

Le Navet Bete is a physical-comedy theatre company based in Exeter, Devon, whose spectacular and hilarious shows have wowed audiences globally since their formation in 2007. The company of five (Al Dunn, Matt Freeman, Dan Bianchi, Nick Bunt and Alex Best) first met each other whilst studying on the Theatre and Performance course at the University of Plymouth in 2003 and, since graduating, have produced fourteen indoor and three outdoor performances to huge critical acclaim and success. Their first two shows *Serendipity* and *Zemblanity*, heavily influenced by bouffon and non-narrative structures, were performed at the Edinburgh Festival Fringe in 2008 and 2009 respectively and gained multiple five-star reviews. As the company developed and grew over the following years, their inimitable style of performance became much more storytelling/narrative-driven with hit shows such as *A Christmas Carol*, *Dick Tracy*, *Dracula: The Bloody Truth*, *Aladdin* and *The Three Musketeers: A Comedy Adventure*, placing physical theatre, fooling and slapstick at the heart of it. With Exeter as their base, they are Associate Artists at the Exeter Northcott Theatre. The company are also Artists in Residence at the Exeter Phoenix and are co-producing partners with the Barbican Theatre, Plymouth, to deliver their annual Christmas show to sell-out audiences every year: *Treasure Island* first premiered at the Plymouth Athenauem in Christmas 2019.

Making accessible work has been at the centre of Le Navet Bete's ethos right from the very beginning. This saw them diversify into outdoor performance in 2010, quickly becoming one of the UK's most ridiculously outrageous, much-loved outdoor acts. They have since performed thousands of outdoor shows from the circus fields at Glastonbury Festival, and the beautiful gardens of the Herrenhausen Palace in Hanover, Germany, to the picturesque Plaza de Armas in Morelia, Mexico, and high up on the side of the Rock of Gibraltar. As well as performing, the company have a widely renowned education programme specialising in clowning, physical comedy, performer–audience relationships and play, that they have taught in schools, colleges and universities across the world from the Royal Central School of Speech and Drama in London to the Universidad Nacional Autonoma de Mexico in Mexico City. *Treasure Island* is Le Navet Bete's seventh collaboration with John Nicholson at the directing helm; the scripts for *Dracula: The Bloody Truth* and *The Three Musketeers: A Comedy Adventure* are both published by Nick Hern Books.

John Nicholson & Le Navet Bete

TREASURE ISLAND

Adapted from the novel
by Robert Louis Stevenson

NICK HERN BOOKS
London
www.nickhernbooks.co.uk

A Nick Hern Book

Treasure Island first published in Great Britain in 2020 as a paperback original by Nick Hern Books Limited, The Glasshouse, 49a Goldhawk Road, London W12 8QP, in association with Le Navet Bete

Treasure Island copyright © 2020 John Nicholson and Le Navet Bete

John Nicholson and Le Navet Bete have asserted their moral right to be identified as the authors of this work

Cover image: Matt Austin

Designed and typeset by Nick Hern Books, London
Printed in the UK by Mimeo Ltd, Huntingdon, Cambridgeshire PE29 6XX

A CIP catalogue record for this book is available from the British Library

ISBN 978 1 84842 983 3

CAUTION All rights whatsoever in this play are strictly reserved. Requests to reproduce the text in whole or in part should be addressed to the publisher.

Amateur Performing Rights Applications for performance, including readings and excerpts, by amateurs throughout the world (excluding the United States of America and Canada) should be addressed to the Performing Rights Manager, Nick Hern Books, The Glasshouse, 49a Goldhawk Road, London W12 8QP, *tel* +44 (0)20 8749 4953, *email* rights@nickhernbooks.co.uk, except as follows:

Australia: ORiGiN Theatrical, Level 1, 213 Clarence Street, Sydney NSW 2000, *tel* +61 (2) 8514 5201, *email* enquiries@originmusic.com.au, *web* www.origintheatrical.com.au

New Zealand: Play Bureau, PO Box 9013, St Clair, Dunedin 9047, *tel* (3) 455 9959, *email* info@playbureau.com

Professional Performing Rights Applications for performance by professionals in any medium and in any language throughout the world (and by amateur and stock companies in the United States of America and Canada) should be addressed to Le Navet Bête c/o Exeter Phoenix Arts Centre, Bradninch Place, Gandy Street, Exeter EX4 3LS, tel. +44 (0) 7849 485770, *email* info@lenavetbete.com

No performance of any kind may be given unless a licence has been obtained. Applications should be made before rehearsals begin. Publication of this play does not necessarily indicate its availability for amateur performance.

Music Companies wishing to listen to or use the music performed in the original production should contact Nick Hern Books in the first instance.

Introduction

John Nicholson, co-writer and director

Treasure Island is an epic, escapist, coming-of-age adventure. It's a big story – and theatrical adaptations tend to employ sizeable casts. This adaptation, however, is written for a cast of four actors, who seamlessly transition between twenty-six characters – so it's certainly epic backstage.

On stage, the action is suspenseful and gripping, as you would expect. But in places it's also irreverent, anarchic and screwball. Despite the fun, it always remains true to the heart and arc of the widely loved novel – this was a very important consideration for us. Naturally, we wanted the adaptation to appeal to a wide age demographic, but within that, we also set about mining the story and characters for comic opportunity. We decided there should be songs, set pieces and an abundance of visual surprises.

Treasure Island is told from the perspective of a fourteen-year-old boy who has to rely on his wits when he's cast into a world of adults. He has to navigate who to trust and who to trick. To this end, although we've streamlined the character list, we've also taken the liberty of including two pivotal characters that Robert Louis Stevenson chose to omit from his original. Or possibly we just invented them.

Stevenson's timeless novel gets pretty graphic in places – murder on the high seas and all that. We were keen not to sanitise these more lurid aspects of the book. We wanted to keep the stakes high, the betrayals wretched, and the danger to life ever present. We also wanted to create characters who were as funny and playful as they were ruthless, as deliciously Machiavellian as they were ridiculous. And finally, we wanted a significant female character – this is a coming-of-age story, after all. This is *Treasure Island* with its heart on its sleeve and its head in a blender.

This production was created with and for the British theatre company Le Navet Bete. A video recording of their production is available for reference purposes. Please feel free to contact them via info@lenavetbete.com. As well as this script, the especially composed music (by Peter Coyte) used in the original production is also available for license.

We hope you enjoy reading – and performing – this adaptation.

This stage adaptation of *Treasure Island* was first performed by Le Navet Bete at the Plymouth Athenaeum on 12 December 2019, and revived at the Exter Northcott Theatre on 9 December 2020. The cast was as follows:

ACTORS	Al Dunn
	Dan Bianchi
	Matt Freeman
	Nick Bunt
Writers/Devisers	Le Navet Bete & John Nicholson
Director	John Nicholson
Lighting Designer and Production Manager	Alex Best
Stage Manager	Abi Jones
Set Designer	Fi Russell
Backdrop Designers	Ben Yates
	Jack Faulkner
	Nic Wootton
	Patrick Hillier
	Riannon Cheffers-Heard
Set Builder	James Andrews
Production Photography	Mark Dawson
Publicity Photography	Matt Austin
Composer and Sound Engineer	Peter Coyte
Graphic Designer	Rebecca Pitt
Wardrobe Assistant	Ruby Yardley
Videographer	Simon Burbage

Characters

PIRATE 1
PIRATE 2
PIRATE 3
PIRATE 4
JIM HAWKINS
AUNT AGNES
PUB CUSTOMER
BILLY BONES
BLIND PEW
HENCHMAN 1
HENCHMAN 2
HENCHMAN 3
DOCKHAND
RACKETEER
SHOE-SHINER
POSH BLOKE
VANESSA
LONG JOHN SILVER
ALEXA THE PARROT,
  a puppet
CAPTAIN BIRDSEYE
BLUE PETER
BLACK DOG
MERMAID
BEN GUNN
CHRISTOPHER
STALLHOLDER
POLICEMAN

And recorded voices of…

FISH 1
FISH 2
JELLYFISH
STARFISH
PLASTIC BAG
GRETA THUNBERG

Suggested Doubling

ACTOR 1: Pirate 3, Jim Hawkins

ACTOR 2: Pirate 2, Pub Customer, Blind Pew, Henchman 2, Racketeer, Long John Silver

ACTOR 3: Pirate 4, Billy Bones, Henchman 3, Posh Bloke, Captain Birdseye, Black Dog, Christopher, Stallholder, Policeman

ACTOR 4: Pirate 1, Aunt Agnes, Henchman 1, Dockhand, Shoe-Shiner, Vanessa, Alexa the Parrot, Blue Peter, Mermaid, Ben Gunn

This text went to press before the end of rehearsals and so may differ slightly from the play as performed.

Scene One

The Burying of the Treasure

A storm. Night. Skeleton Island. PIRATE 1 *and* PIRATE 2 *are digging.*

PIRATE 1. Surely this is deep enough.

PIRATE 2. Keep digging.

PIRATE 1. I am keeping digging. You keep digging.

PIRATE 2. I am keeping digging.

PIRATE 1. Fine. So how deep do we go?

PIRATE 2. No idea.

PIRATE 1. Oh great. So we could even be too deep!?

PIRATE 2. How the hell should I know?!

PIRATE 1. You bilge rat!

PIRATE 2. No, *you're* a bilge rat!

PIRATE 1. No, you're a…

PIRATE 3 (*off*). Oi, swabs! Is that hole the specified depth yet?

   PIRATE 1 *and* PIRATE 2 *exchange a look.*

PIRATES 1 *and* 2. Aye!

PIRATE 4. Then let's get lowering.

   A treasure chest is belayed above the audience towards the stage. PIRATE 1 *and* PIRATE 2 *grab lines to bring it in.*

PIRATE 1. You're bringing a spring upon her cable, swab!

PIRATE 3. Come about, you fools!

PIRATE 4. No, belay to the left!

PIRATE 2. Whose left?

PIRATE 4. There'll be *none* of us left if we don't hurry.

PIRATE 3. Furl, swabs! She's heaving down.

The chest lurches and some of the chest's contents (money) showers into the audience.

PIRATE 2. Hold fast!

PIRATE 4. We're all for the Davy Jones if the chest is delivered to the waves!

PIRATE 1. Slacken off the guideline. Gently does it!

PIRATE 2. A few more feet to terra firma.

PIRATE 1. She's safe!

PIRATE 1 and PIRATE 2 set about lowering the chest into the hole.

PIRATE 4. Now lay her to rest and don't dawdle. Be there a cartographer among us?

PIRATE 2. A car-what-a-pher?

PIRATE 1. A map drawer, numbskull! Captain Flint's ordered a map to mark the treasure's whereabouts.

PIRATE 3. Leave that to me.

PIRATE 2. We'll make the ground good and mark the site with an 'X'?

PIRATE 3. Job's a good 'un.

PIRATE 1. An 'X'? Brilliant. Really original.

PIRATE 2. A 'T' then.

PIRATE 3. 'T' for Treasure.

PIRATE 1. Inspired. Tell you what, why don't you put a massive sign up that reads 'Treasure buried here'. You know – just to avoid any confusion.

PIRATE 3. What's with the salty attitude?

PIRATE 1. Does it not occur to you that the whereabouts of this treasure has to be disguised! Only cryptic clues upon a map should lead to its hiding place.

PIRATES 2 *and* 3. Ahh.

PIRATE 4. And until such a time as her resurrection shares us our fortune.

PIRATE 1. Should Flint keep her word, that is.

PIRATE 4. What do you mean by that?

PIRATE 1. Well, do you trust her?

Sudden change in atmosphere.

PIRATE 2. Anyone else sensing there are eyes out there upon us?

PIRATE 3. Many pairs of 'em an' all.

A figure appears in the shadows in a long coat and wide-brimmed hat.

PIRATE 2. Captain Flint! Where did you come from?

'FLINT'. I think the most important question right now, swabs, is *not* whether you trust *me*, but whether I trust *you*. And unfortunately for you, I don't.

She raises two guns and kills the four men. Black out. 'Treasure Island' theme plays.

Scene Two

Hard Times

JIM HAWKINS *is stood in a spotlight, lost in thought, with the sound of adventure in his ears. But a voice is calling him back to reality, distant at first but getting louder.*

AUNT AGNES. Nephew. Nephew. Nephew. Nephew!!!

Reality. The Admiral Benbow. Black Hill Cove. It's not a night you'd want to be outside. The elements blow in through an open door. AUNT AGNES is sat in a chair by the fire.

AUNT AGNES. Will you close that blessed door!

JIM. I'm sorry, Aunt Agnes.

JIM *does so then tends to the fire with the logs he's brought in.*

AUNT AGNES. Are you *literally* trying to freeze me to death!?

JIM. No, Aunt.

AUNT AGNES. After the way I've cared for you all these years?

JIM. It shouldn't take too long to warm up now.

AUNT AGNES. Nothing but a thorn in my side you've been since your parents chose to abandon you.

JIM. I don't think it was their intention to die.

AUNT AGNES. Expecting old muggins here to step in and run this pub.

JIM. I thought you had nowhere else to live?

AUNT AGNES. Selfish. The pair of them. No other word for it.

JIM. Well, I'm fourteen now, so...

AUNT AGNES. So you want to kick me out into the gutter, is that it?

JIM. No! I wasn't going to say that.

AUNT AGNES. It's what you were thinking, though, isn't it, you ungrateful little haemorrhoid.

JIM (*to audience*). Believe me, this is a *good* day. Sometimes she can be quite cruel.

JIM *busies himself at the bar.*

AUNT AGNES. If only he had a bit of sense about him. But alas, there's nothing but a chasm of soft soap between his ears. He believes in mermaids, you know.

JIM. Aunt!

AUNT AGNES. It's true. You're a dreamer. Nothing but a dreamer. Well, can you put your hands on your head? Oh no! Super! Tramp all over me in the meantime.

JIM. I need to change the barrels.

JIM *heads down into the trap/cellar.*

AUNT AGNES. You and your feckless ways are driving this business into the ground, you know.

PUB CUSTOMER *enters, battling to shut the door against the howling wind.*

PUB CUSTOMER. Blimey, what a night. Any chance of a pint?

AUNT AGNES (*hurling her knitting needles at him*). No! Get out of my pub!!

PUB CUSTOMER *swiftly exits.*

(*To audience, re: JIM.*) Oh, don't you take his side. That snivelling little brat down there changed the course of my life. I could have been a model once. You can see that, can't you, sir? (*Threateningly points a fire poker at an audience member.*) I said, you can see that can't you?! What's your name?

The audience member says their name. JIM *emerges from the cellar.*

Nephew, pour me a double rum and raw egg – keeps me regular – and whatever [*audience member's name*] wants.

JIM (*sotto to audience member*). Listen – as long as you don't come up here, you're safe, okay?

AUNT AGNES. Did he just tell you not to come up here?

Upstage, JIM *gestures for them to say 'no'.*

AUNT AGNES. Good. Hurry up with those drinks! We need a proper man about the place.

JIM. I've actually thought of an idea to raise some additional income.

AUNT AGNES. So have I: kill yourself so I can flog ya body to medical science.

JIM. Very funny, Aunt. I could rent out my room.

AUNT AGNES. And where will you sleep? In the dog basket?

JIM. Perhaps. Well, until Lucky comes home...

He looks sadly at the empty dog basket.

AUNT AGNES. Oh Jim, I don't think he will. Cos he's dead!!

JIM. Look, I've made up an advert. (*Picking up leaflet.*) I thought I'd stick it here in the window.

Just as he does exactly that, the front door bursts open.

Scene Three

The Arrival of Bones

A heaving great man stands in the doorway with a luggage trunk on his shoulder.

BILLY BONES. I've come about the room.

AUNT AGNES. Oh my.

BILLY BONES. Bed, rum and eatables covers all my requirements.

He slams his trunk down.

But not necessarily in that order.

JIM. Right. So...

BILLY BONES *walks menacingly towards* JIM.

BILLY BONES. Figure it out, girl.

JIM. Boy, actually.

BILLY BONES *quickly scans the place for vantage points – he's expecting trouble.*

Actually, you know what –

BILLY BONES. I'll take it. How much?

AUNT AGNES. Four shillings a night.

JIM. You see, the thing is, Mr...

BILLY BONES. Bones. Billy Bones.

JIM. I'm afraid the room isn't actually available any more. Isn't that right, Aunt Agnes?

AUNT AGNES. What are you talking about, you twonk? Money up front – you understand, of course.

BILLY BONES. Course.

AUNT AGNES. Much obliged. Now take his trunk upstairs and be quick about it.

JIM. Yes, Aunt.

JIM *goes to take the trunk.* BILLY BONES *spins round and throttles* JIM *up against the bar.*

BILLY BONES. Now don't you ever be touching that trunk, you hear me?!

JIM. Yes! Whatever you say.

BILLY BONES. Good. I need a drink.

He sits at a table.

AUNT AGNES. Nephew! Get him a drink.

BILLY BONES *slams a few gold pieces on the table.*

BILLY BONES. That should see me through to the end of the week.

BILLY BONES *takes the drink.* JIM *looks at the money – the inn needs it.*

AUNT AGNES. Leave it! (*Gets up and takes the money for herself.*) Your room's next to mine, Mr Boner.

JIM. Bones!

BILLY BONES. Another.

JIM *pours.*

Now then, girl.

JIM. Boy.

BILLY BONES (*producing his knife*). I'll be needing your eyes.

JIM. What!?

AUNT AGNES. I'm sure we can come to an arrangement about that too.

JIM. Shut up, Aunt.

BILLY BONES. I want you to watch the road like an 'awk – thiswards for suspicious-looking sea vessels, thatwards for toothless vagabonds, and everywards for a deceptively rum… unidexter.

JIM. A what?

BILLY BONES. Nothing but thin air resides below his left knee.

JIM. You mean…

BILLY BONES. By his own hand, story goes.

JIM (*to himself, in horror*). He cut off his own leg?

BILLY BONES. It's too quiet around here. Makes me nervous. You play that thing?

Motions to a harpsichord.

JIM. Only occasionally. Just the odd song to try and attract trade.

AUNT AGNES. Thank Christ. He's about as musical as a poo landing on a drum.

   BILLY BONES *waggles his fingers towards* JIM – *motioning him to play.*

JIM. Right. Well, I'm working on a new one actually. For Dad. I never really knew him but my mum told me folk would come from miles around to listen to his tales. And you know what, sometimes… (*Off Bones's look.*) I'll just play it.

He plays the Cheers *theme song ('Where Everybody Knows Your Name' by Gary Portay and Judy Hart-Angelo). [NB. An alternative song may be used.]* BILLY BONES *listens in stunned silence before heading towards* JIM, *knife in hand. When* JIM *reaches the chorus,* BILLY BONES *smashes the harpsichord lid down before forcing* JIM*'s hands repeatedly down on the keys whilst singing…*

BILLY BONES. *Fifteen men on a dead man's chest*
Yo ho ho and a bottle of rum
Drink and the devil had done for the rest
Yo ho ho and a bottle of rum.

Well, what can I say, it's been a lovely evening. And now for my Uncle Ned.

JIM. It's upstairs just along…

BILLY BONES. I'll find it, girl.

JIM. Boy.

BILLY BONES. And remember – thiswards, thatwards and everywards.

He takes the bottle from the bar and exits with his trunk.

JIM (*after him*). Right. But if you want to take the whole bottle you'll need to –

BILLY BONES. *Fifteen men on a dead man's chest.*

JIM. – pay first.

AUNT AGNES. What have you done now, nephew!? Better get in your basket.

She blows out a lamp. Transition. JIM *stands in a spotlight, looking.*

JIM. Thiswards, thatwards and everywards. Thiswards, thatwards and everywards!

Until…

AUNT AGNES. Three weeks' debt to us now and nothing forthcoming. He's bleeding us dry. What have you done, nephew?

JIM. I'll talk to him!

BILLY BONES *enters and heads to his table.*

BILLY BONES. Rum!

JIM. Yes, Mr Bones. I do need to point out, though, you're running up quite a tab.

BILLY BONES. You saying you don't trust me to pay my way?

AUNT AGNES. The insolence of the boy. Deserves a good hiding.

She exits.

JIM. I'm saying we're down to our last bottle of rum.

BILLY BONES. Send it over and you have my word I'll pay ye what I owes.

JIM. Very well. But only if you also agree to answer a few questions.

BILLY BONES. What kinda questions, boy?

JIM. Girl. I mean boy! Why do I have to look thiswards and thatwards and everywards all the time?

BILLY BONES. Cos there's bad people in the world. Badder 'n me. Drink!

JIM pours him a glass, which he downs.

JIM. What do these people want?

BILLY BONES. I'm telling you nothing.

JIM offers him the bottle.

Okay, give me the bottle and I'll tell you everything. (*Snatches it out of* JIM's *hand.*) They want that trunk upstairs.

JIM. Why? Does it belong to them?

BILLY BONES. No! It was entrusted to me by a woman called Flint, before she died.

JIM. So… what's so special about it?

BILLY BONES. You don't need to know that.

JIM draws up a stool.

JIM. But who are these… 'bad people'? Where do they come from?

BILLY BONES. Drawn together from across oceans – like famished rats to a freshly made corpse – screeching and ripping at each other to be the first to gorge. The wickedest men that God ever allowed in a boat.

JIM. Blimey.

BILLY BONES. But there's one that surpasses them all.

JIM. The man with one leg?

BILLY BONES. No. Another. Never in your life will you see a more dreadful-looking figure.

JIM. You've met him?

BILLY BONES. No one has.

JIM. Then how do you know –

BILLY BONES. Because! We've all seen what he can do. Thems that die before he can get to 'em are the lucky ones.

He starts to exit.

JIM. Does he have a name?

BILLY BONES. Aye. But no man ever dare utter it.

JIM. What is it?

BILLY BONES. The Raven.

He exits, leaving JIM *alone, sat at the table.*

Scene Four

The Arrival of Blind Pew

Tension mounts. As does a tap-tapping. JIM *looks, horrified, towards the door, which flies open. Phew – it's just an old man with a walking stick.*

BLIND PEW. Hello? Could anyone with half a heart inform an old blind man of his whereabouts?

JIM. The Admiral Benbow, Black Hill Cove.

BLIND PEW. Much obliged. Now please, lend me your arm, I need to sit.

JIM. Of course, come this way.

As JIM *leads him in,* BLIND PEW *suddenly pulls* JIM*'s arm behind his back and into a crippling hold.*

BLIND PEW. Now tell me the whereabouts of one Billy Bones or I snap it at the elbow.

BILLY BONES *appears from the shadows.*

BILLY BONES. Let the sapling go, Blind Pew.

BLIND PEW. Hello, Bones. You thought you could hide from us, didn't you? But I'd know your stench from a continent away.

BILLY BONES. How did you find me?

BLIND PEW. I've just told you – you stink. It's the end of the line. No more running. Now, hand over Flint's Fist. Come on, Bones, the boy's in pain. (*Twisting* JIM*'s arm.*)

JIM. Arghhh!

BILLY BONES. It's hidden. You'll never find it.

BLIND PEW. Don't lie. It's upstairs.

BILLY BONES. How did you know that?

BLIND PEW. I didn't.

BILLY BONES. Arghhh! Take this, you dog!

He throws a knife at BLIND PEW, *who catches it with lightning-fast reflexes.* JIM *escapes behind the harpsichord. A violent fight ensues, during which* BLIND PEW *places something into* BILLY BONES' *hand.*

No. The Black Spot! No!

BLIND PEW. You could have made this so much easier for yourself.

BILLY BONES. I refuse it!

He slaps the Black Spot onto the table.

BLIND PEW. You know as well as I, it's too late for that. (*To* JIM.) You – fetch his trunk.

BILLY BONES. Do what he says. Save yourself. It's over.

JIM. But how…?

BILLY BONES. How long do I have?

BLIND PEW. A matter of minutes.

JIM. But hang on! This is just an ink splodge on a bit of paper.

BLIND PEW. Is it!?

JIM. Well… yes.

BLIND PEW. Yet there's never a man who's received it and seen a good day a'terward.

BILLY BONES. Once passed from one to another, it marks your end.

JIM. Blimey. Quite a weapon then.

BLIND PEW. Deadly.

JIM. Well, in that case, you'd better have it back, Mr Pew.

BLIND PEW. Much obliged.

He takes it.

JIM. From me to you.

BLIND PEW. What? Oh crap. How long do I have?

BILLY BONES. Timing's up to you, Jim.

JIM. Three seconds?

BLIND PEW *drops the Black Spot and dies.* AUNT AGNES *enters.* JIM *picks up the Black Spot.*

AUNT AGNES. What the hell is going on here? Who's he? (*Gesturing to* BLIND PEW.) And what's that?

JIM. Nothing. Aunt Agnes, can I suggest you stay out of the way?

AUNT AGNES. No. What's that in your hand?

JIM. It's honestly nothing.

AUNT AGNES. Well, it's clearly not nothing. Hand it over.

JIM. Seriously! Just walk away.

She pulls out a gun and aims it at JIM.

AUNT AGNES. Say another word and it'll be your final act of defiance. Now give me whatever's in your hand.

JIM (*to audience*). Should I?

JIM *hands* AUNT AGNES *the Black Spot. She immediately dies.*

BILLY BONES. There'll be more to arrive soon. Save yourself. Here, take the key to my trunk and...

JIM. And what?

BILLY BONES *dies.*

And what!? Oh God! Aunt Agnes!

He looks down at her and tries to cry.

Nope, it's not coming. The trunk!

He covers the bodies with a blanket then rushes upstairs with a lamp.

Scene Five

The Opening of Bones' Trunk

JIM. Whatever's in here, people are prepared to kill for it. I should just leave it. Or maybe this could be the start of a most epic journey. Should I open it? Maybe there's an answer out there in the wind?

He looks out.

AUDIENCE. Open it.

JIM. Here goes.

He inserts the key and lifts the lid. He pulls out bizarre objects until he reaches the bottom and finds... a single gold coin.

That's it!?

Deflated, he turns away.

Or maybe...

He opens the trunk again, rips into the lid lining and pulls out... some documents.

What on earth is this?

Voices in the dark below.

HENCHMAN 3 (*off*). You two, tear the place apart – and anyone else you need to, until Flint's Fist is secure. Go. The rest of you – surround the building and keep your torches lit. There'll be no hiding place.

Two men enter the inn (bodies of BILLY BONES, BLIND PEW *and* AUNT AGNES *have been replaced with 'doubles' under the blanket).*

HENCHMAN 1. Three bodies.

HENCHMAN 2. Dead?

HENCHMAN 1. Reckon.

HENCHMAN 2. Well, stick a knife in 'em to know!

HENCHMAN 1. This one's Pew. Still warm.

HENCHMAN 2. And if I'm not mistaken by the stench – here's Bones.

HENCHMAN 1. And the hag?

HENCHMAN 2. Who cares. But this ain't looking good.

HENCHMAN 1. Upstairs?

HENCHMAN 2. Go.

JIM shoves the documents into his waistcoat and hides.

HENCHMAN 1. The chest. It's been opened.

HENCHMAN 2. Is it there? Is the Fist there!!?

HENCHMAN 1. Too late! Someone's been before us! (*Picks up* JIM*'s lamp.*) Recently extinguished. He won't have got far.

HENCHMAN 2. Then through hell's gates with him, if he be!

HENCHMAN 1. Turn the hovel over!

HENCHMAN 2. Search the surroundings and leave no stone unturned!

Murderous cries fill the air. The house is being torn apart (scene change). JIM *makes his escape from the inn and runs for his life. When he slows, he hears voices above him.*

HENCHMAN 1. Anything?

HENCHMAN 2. Nothing.

HENCHMAN 3 (*off*). You two. Call it in. We're not safe exposed like this. Boss wants the dead disappeared from the inn before light. We set sail at dawn. Understood?

HENCHMAN 1. Aye.

HENCHMAN 2. Aye.

HENCHMAN 1. You think this is the work of…

HENCHMAN 2. The Raven? I'd bet my life on it. And yours too.

HENCHMAN 1. Maybe he's among us.

HENCHMAN 2. Maybe you're the Raven.

HENCHMAN 1. Maybe you're the Raven.

HENCHMAN 2. You'd be dead if I was.

HENCHMAN 1. You'd be double-dead if I was.

HENCHMAN 2. Shut it! Let's get back to the ship.

JIM is left alone.

JIM. What have I done? What is this? What is Flint's Fist?

He opens the document.

A map?

It has 'Treasure Map' written on the back of it. He turns it around.

A treasure map!!

Rain. He covers himself and sinks to the floor, falling asleep from exhaustion. Transition into a bright, crisp morning.

Scene Six

The Deal at the Docks

A dockyard. A DOCKHAND *walks past carrying a crate of apples on his shoulders.*

DOCKHAND. Come on, lads, let's get these apples 'n' pears up the apples 'n' pears. Oh, I crack myself up sometimes.

JIM *steals an apple off a crate but the* DOCKHAND *grabs it back off him.*

Oi! Cheeky scamp!

JIM *checks his surroundings, then sits and pulls out the map.*

JIM. I've seen other maps from sailors at The Admiral Benbow who've sailed these waters before. I reckon this island has to be in the Caribbean. But how am I, a fourteen-year-old lad from Devon, going to sail to the Caribbean and look for treasure?! I've not even crossed the Tamar! And this coin's all I have in the world.

A RACKETEER *walks in on this line and looks to take advantage with his dodgy 'ball-under-the-cup' game.*

RACKETEER. All right, folks, chase the lady, chase the lady. Just follow the ball and tell me which cup it's under. How about placing a bet, sir? I'll double your money if you win.

JIM *looks at his coin and places it on the table.*

Okay, here we go, chase the lady, chase the lady. Now, which cup is it under?

JIM. The left one.

RACKETEER. I don't think you mean that, though, do you? You clearly saw it go under the middle one.

JIM. Well, I agree that's what you wanted me to see. But you would've switched it.

RACKETEER. Are you accusing me of cheating? Are you accusing me of cheating!?

He breaks into song. A SHOE-SHINER *enters to shine a* POSH BLOKE's *shoes. They become the chorus line.*

I'm not a cheat
I should knock you off your feet
I'm a racketeer, let's make that clear

CHORUS. *He's a racketeer, let's make that clear.*

RACKETEER. *I might duck and dive*
Just to try to survive
But I must repeat, I'm not a cheat

CHORUS. *He must repeat he's not a cheat.*

Mouth-organ solo.

RACKETEER. *You can call me a cheeky chappie*

CHORUS. *He won't resent that name*

RACKETEER. *And I might just pull a fast one*
But cheating's not my game.

CHORUS. *He's a racketeer, let's give him a cheer*

RACKETEER. *I might look queer but there's nothing to fear*

CHORUS. *He's just…*

RACKETEER. *A little bit of this and a little bit of that,*
And a little bit dodgy

CHORUS. *And a little bit fat.*

RACKETEER. Oi!

JIM. I don't care! The fact is, you owe me double the value of my coin. (*Takes back his original coin.*)

RACKETEER. Get out of here, kid.

JIM. Give me my winnings!

POSH BLOKE. What's going on here?

RACKETEER. Kid wants to gamble. But he's got no assets.

JIM. I have. The Admiral Benbow, above Black Hill Cove. I own it.

POSH BLOKE. Is that so? I've always fancied owning an inn. Beer on tap, 24/7. What say you put your inn up against… Oh, I don't know. One of my ships? That one.

JIM. The schooner!?

POSH BLOKE. Why not?

RACKETEER. You really gonna risk your pub on some boat, lad?

POSH BLOKE. I'll have you know, that isn't just *some boat*. It's a fully stocked, high-spec, 1740, best-in-its-class, three-mast schooner. So, what'll it be? Black Jack? Poker?

JIM. Higher Lower.

POSH BLOKE. As in… *Play Your Cards Right*?

JIM. Yeah. Unless you want to back out?

POSH BLOKE. Let's play!

RACKETEER. Let's play!

Curtains open to reveal a game-show set with two lines of five large playing cards on a vertical board (ten cards in total, face down). A glamorous assistant, VANESSA, stands beside it. RACKETEER is now sporting a gold sparkly jacket.

Good evening, folks, and welcome to *Play Your Cards Right*. And this week we're playing for a pub and a ship!

AUDIENCE. Wooo!

RACKETEER. This is my beautiful assistant, Vanessa. Give us a twirl, Vanessa. Doesn't she look lovely, everyone? So, let's meet our contestants. Contestant number one, what's your name and where are you from?

JIM. My name's Jim Hawkins and I'm from Devon.

RACKETEER. Contestant number two, what's your name and where do you come from?

POSH BLOKE. Bartholomew the 4th and I'm from Bath.

RACKETEER. Okay then! Let's play... *Play Your Cards Right*!

Game-show theme tune.

Now then, Bartholomew, you're up first and your first card is a...

VANESSA *turns cards.*

VANESSA. Nine!

RACKETEER. Now, what do you think, folks, is the next card higher or lower than a nine, call it out, what do you think?

Audience shout out 'Higher' or 'Lower' each round.

POSH BLOKE. Higher.

VANESSA *turns the card.*

VANESSA. It's a Jack!

RACKETEER. Well done, Bartholomew. Now, Jim, your first card is a...

VANESSA. Five!

RACKETEER. What do we think, folks?

JIM. Higher.

VANESSA. It's a ten!

RACKETEER. Well played. Now, back to Bartholomew. You're on a Jack. Higher or lower than a Jack?

POSH BLOKE. Lower.

VANESSA. It's a six!

RACKETEER. You're safe for now. Jim, back to you. You're on a ten.

JIM. Lower.

VANESSA. It's a four!

RACKETEER. Bartholomew is on a six, where are you going from there?

POSH BLOKE. Higher.

RACKETEER. You're going higher and it's…

VANESSA. An eight!

RACKETEER. Jim, higher or lower than a four? What do we think, folks?

JIM. It's got to be higher.

RACKETEER. Vanessa?

VANESSA. It's a… seven!

RACKETEER. Right then, Bartholomew, final card, you're on an eight and there's all to play for, where are you going to go?

POSH BLOKE. Lower.

VANESSA. It's a King!

RACKETEER. Oh, unlucky. I'm sorry. Now, Jim. We know about the pub, it's safe, it's in the bank. But to win the ship, is the next card higher or lower than a seven?

JIM. I can't decide on my own! I'm going to nominate… (*To someone on front row.*) you!

RACKETEER. Very well, up you come then, madam. What's your name and where do you come from?

The volunteer answers.

Sorry?

The volunteer repeats their answer.

No, I heard you, I'm just sorry! Okay, Anna, the next voice you hear will be mine. Now then, for the ship and for the sake of the rest of the show, are you going to go higher or lower than a seven?

Drum roll. The volunteer guesses.

Are you sure? Are you absolutely convinced? Do you want to change your mind?

If they do…

Are you sure? Are you absolutely convinced? Do you want to change your mind?

The card is rigged so JIM *wins whichever way volunteer calls it.*

Vanessa, she's gone higher! Is the next card higher than a seven…!?

VANESSA. It's an eight!

RACKETEER. He wins! Jim Hawkins, you keep your dignity, you keep your inn, and you win that flipping great schooner out there in the dock. And for you, Bartholomew, you go home with our runner-up prize – an all-expenses-paid trip to Skegness.

VANESSA *offers an envelope, which he refuses.*

POSH BLOKE (*exiting*). Stuff this!

RACKETEER. Well, it looks like me and Vanessa are off for a romantic weekend in Skeggy.

VANESSA. Are you gonna tell your wife this time?

RACKETEER. Ha-ha! Good one, Vanessa. Anyway, see you all next time when we play *Play Your Cards Right*!

They exit. JIM *turns and walks towards his ship.*

Scene Seven

Recruiting the Crew

JIM. Oh. My. God. It's mine! I own a ship called…

A sign pops up with a comic sound effect.

The Jolly Todger? Oh well. She's beautiful. I'm the luckiest
boy I know.

He climbs aboard and sings.

I used to think nothing would happen
To me that was good.
But suddenly now I own a ship
Built out of plywood.
The feeling I have now inside me
Is hard to contain.
What's happened to me just since last night
Oh man, it's insane.

I'm walking on sunshine (whoa!)
I'm walking on sunshine (whoa!)
I'm walking on sunshine (whoa!)
Oh man, I'm feelin' good!

Hey, all right now
And I've gotta find a crew!

But *how* am I going to find a crew?

*He starts to head back to the dock when there's muffled
shouting and thumping from below him. He descends and
opens the trap. A barrel bobs up.*

What the… Don't worry, I'll get you out, hold on!

He pulls off the lid. LONG JOHN SILVER (SILVER) *pops
up, spits out a mouthful of seawater and grabs* JIM.

SILVER. What dock be this, boy?

JIM. Avonmouth. Bristol.

SILVER. Well, how's about that!? I win, you blaggards!

JIM. Win what?

SILVER. A bet. To cross the Atlantic in a barrel.

JIM. Ha! I don't believe you've done that.

SILVER. Wise lad. I wouldn't either. Truth is, I was hiding.

JIM. Who from?

SILVER. A very amorous selkie.

JIM. A mermaid!?

SILVER. No, selkies are seal women who shed their skin and walk on land. Mermaids are forever sea-bound.

JIM. Unless they give up their sea life.

SILVER. Yep, but I never met one who was prepared to.

JIM. You've met a mermaid?

SILVER. Plenty! But look at us, we haven't even introduced ourshelves... our *shelves*? I've got two of them at home in me kitchen! Most people know me as Long John Silver.

JIM. And the others?

SILVER. There are no others.

A parrot on a stick enters, with a flashing LED round its neck, operated by Actor 4.

A-ha! I wondered when you'd turn up. And this 'ere be Alexa. Say something, Alexa.

ALEXA. I'm trying to connect.

SILVER. Yeah, quelle surprise!

JIM. A talking parrot. Wow! Where did you get her?

SILVER. The Amazon, of course. Now, I didn't catch your name.

ALEXA exits.

JIM. Jim Hawkins.

SILVER. Well then, Jim lad, lend me your shoulder and help me outta this thing.

JIM *does so and then looks in horror at his leg.*

Not many advantages to having a... (*Taps it three times.*) wooden leg. And getting out of barrels certainly ain't one of 'em.

JIM. How did you – ?

SILVER. Lose it? Now there's a yarnful tale. A run-in with a giant off the Peloponnese coast.

JIM. A giant?

SILVER. Had it in a single bite, he did. Before I managed to row away in one of his teacups. Well, I'd best be on me way.

JIM. Where to?

SILVER. To have more adventures! Just need to find a ship.

JIM. I have a ship.

SILVER. Yeah right.

JIM. I do. This schooner. I just won her in a card game.

SILVER. Well, ain't she a beaut, Alexa? *The Jolly Todger.*

ALEXA *crosses.*

ALEXA. Searching for images of 'todger'?

SILVER. No!!

ALEXA *exits.*

But what would a lad like you be wanting with a ship like this?

JIM. Adventure.

SILVER. And where do you think you might find that?

JIM. I was thinking... the Caribbean.

SILVER. Interesting. What draws your interest there?

JIM. Nothing! Nothing at all. I just heard it was a good... holiday destination.

SILVER. A Devonshire lad in 1757, smart as paint, decides to embark on a Caribbean cruise in a ship he's just won in a card game?

JIM. Correct.

SILVER. And you think my stories sound implausible!

JIM. Mr Silver, I imagine you've sailed the Caribbean waters before.

SILVER. Over more than one lifetime, feels like.

JIM. In that case, would you be willing to captain *The Jolly Todger*?

SILVER. Ha! I'm no captain. Not high enough born. I'm merely a ship's cook.

JIM. Then will you be my ship's cook? Please. The truth is, I have no one else to turn to for help.

SILVER. That so? Well, I'll have to cogitate on that proposal with a considerable amount of thought.

JIM. I'm in a bit of a hurry.

SILVER. I accept. I'll offer my services for food, board and just the occasional grog. And if it's of interest...

JIM. It probably will be.

SILVER. I might happen to know one or two very reliable crew hands.

JIM. I can't quite believe all this is happening! Now we just need a captain.

Enter a man who's the spit of CAPTAIN BIRDSEYE *from the nineties TV advert.*

Well, if luck comes in threes!

SILVER. Jim, that's something we don't want to rush into. You should leave that up to me!

JIM. Excuse me, sir, you wouldn't happen to be a ship's captain, would you?

BIRDSEYE. Well yes, as a matter of fact I am, young man! Captain Birdseye. Honoured to meet your acquaintance. Fish finger?

He offers JIM *a fish finger from a paper bag.*

JIM. A finger made from fish?

BIRDSEYE. With a roasted breadcrumb coating. Only the best for the captain's table. What do you think?

JIM. Honestly? A bit dry. They'd probably fusion well with some haricot beans immersed in a rich tomato sauce.

BIRDSEYE. My God! Fishfingers and beans. I could dominate children's cuisine forever.

SILVER (*sotto*). Wait, Jim. We know nothing about him.

JIM (*sotto*). Apart from the fact that he looks like the Santa of the Sea – what's not to like? Captain Birdseye, my friend and I are in need of a captain to sail *The Jolly Todger* across the Atlantic to the Caribbean.

BIRDSEYE. Indeed. And have you a crew?

SILVER. I'm the cook. And I'm in charge of the crew.

BIRDSEYE. And you are…?

SILVER. Most people know me as Long John Silver.

BIRDSEYE. And the others?

SILVER. There are no others.

JIM. Please, Captain Birdseye. I can't imagine a captain more suitable than you.

BIRDSEYE. Very well then. I accept. I'll meet you here at dawn to set sail. Do we have an accord?

JIM. Oh yes, sir… Captain! See you here at dawn.

BIRDSEYE. Bright-eyed and fishy-tailed.

He exits.

SILVER. Interesting.

JIM. How on earth was all that so easy!? I really am the luckiest boy alive!

SILVER. We only have until morning to recruit a crew. So, Jim, you best get settled in.

JIM. But I'd quite like to –

SILVER. No you wouldn't, now off you go to get some rest.

He forces JIM *off.*

Scene Eight

Setting Off

SILVER. Blue Peter? Blue Peter?

BLUE PETER *enters in tight white shorts and cropped top.*

BLUE PETER. I've told you: it's Pierre le Bleu.

SILVER. *What* are you wearing?

BLUE PETER. Jean Paul Gaultier. Do you like it?

SILVER. No, it's proper weird. Where's Black Dog?

BLUE PETER. On his way. Any news?

SILVER. We're on.

BLUE PETER. I'm impressed. So where are we headed?

SILVER. The Caribbean.

BLUE PETER. Ooh la la!

SILVER. All right, calm down. Remember, you're under *my* orders. Clear?

BLUE PETER. As a whistle. (*Toots a flourish on his penny whistle.*)

SILVER. Good. We'll need a crew sufficient in numbers. Reckon you swabs can organise that?

BLACK DOG *enters.*

Well, glad you could finally join us, Black Dog.

BLACK DOG. Leave it with us, boss.

They address the audience.

Right, listen up. Which of you landlubbing scallywags wants to join our crew? But no trouble-makers or you'll be walking the plank. Over to you, Blue Peter.

BLUE PETER. I need four children and three strong adults – [*etc.*]

BLUE PETER *hands out hats and brings seven audience members up on stage.* SILVER *lines them up.* [*NB. This section can be adapted to accommodate less audience interaction, if required.*]

We have our crew!

JIM *enters.*

SILVER. Morning, Jim. Let me introduce you to the crew who'll be assisting to deliver your Caribbean dream. None of them pretty to look at but men and women by their faces. This one 'ere's Light-Fingered Linda – cos she likes thieving. You'll be on spud-peeling.

BLUE PETER *leads them to their jobs as they get introduced by* SILVER.

And here we have Bum-Face Bill – no explanation needed. You're on knots.

Led off to untie knots.

This is Recycling Roy – for obvious reasons. Right, sock-pairing. Off you go, Roy.

Led off to pair socks.

This one's Simple Susan, here's Cloth-Eared Clive, that's Roger the Rogerer.

They are assigned mopping, scrubbing and sewing sacks.

And last but not least, here's Mucky Mike [*or Melinda*]. Tell everyone how you got your name, Mucky Mike. And keep it clean.

If they don't immediately come up with an answer…

Ha-ha! He can't keep it clean!

BIRDSEYE *enters on the top deck of the ship.*

BIRDSEYE. Are we a full complement?

SILVER. We are, Captain Birdseye!

BIRDSEYE. Then raise the anchor and hoist the mainsail!

JIM *and Mucky Mike pull on the rope to hoist the sail and the ship sets sail. Epic music.* BIRDSEYE *is at the wheel and the crew work.*

JIM. We're sailing!

BLUE PETER *stands at the front of the boat and gets* JIM *to hold him (à la* Titanic *film image).* SILVER *sends* BLUE PETER *back to work.*

BIRDSEYE. Silver?

SILVER. Aye, Captain Birdseye.

BIRDSEYE. We've made it out into calm waters. Should be plain sailing for a while now.

SILVER. Very well. (*To onstage audience members.*) You swabs can scram back to your bunks and get rested up for a while.

BLUE PETER *leads them back to their seats.*

I'm off to knock up some scran. We'll fill our bellies tonight.

BIRDSEYE. No scran for me, Silver. There's a pack o' fish fingers below deck with my name on it.

SILVER. Right. Ta-ta.

BIRDSEYE. No, I prefer ketchup. Only the best for the captain's table.

JIM *climbs to the top deck and sits alone.*

Scene Nine

Getting to Know You

Scene turns to night. JIM *checks his surroundings before producing his treasure map.*

JIM (*reads*). 'Below the yellow fingers, two steps of a civilian, and six feet below… ten thousand million.'

ALEXA *approaches.* JIM *hurriedly places the map in a suitable hiding place.*

Oh hey, Alexa. Have you ever seen a night that's finer?

ALEXA. Searching for 'lights in China'.

JIM. What?

ALEXA (*exiting*). Purchasing Chinese lanterns.

SILVER *enters.*

SILVER. Alexa! What are you ordering now!? The amount of crap that gets delivered to me. All right, Jim lad. Grub's nearly up. Everything all right?

JIM. I was just wondering what it'll be like when we get there.

SILVER *joins him.*

SILVER. Like paradise. Climbing, swimming, diving into clear blue water.

JIM. Really?

SILVER. Barbecues, hunting, fishing, stories around the fire at night.

A shooting star.

And what a night, eh?

JIM. All those stars.

SILVER. More stars in the universe than all the grains of sand on all the beaches of the world combined.

JIM. What, really?

SILVER. Oh yes. You could travel for billions of years at the speed of light and still be surrounded by 'em. But that one there – the pole star – that's our friend.

JIM. Why?

SILVER. Cos she never moves. All the rest appear to circle to us, but she stays rooted to the spot. So, she's our mapping point, see. You any good with maps?

JIM. I like looking at the ones Captain Birdseye reads from.

SILVER. Takes experience before they come into focus.

JIM. Do you understand them?

SILVER. Maps, cryptic crosswords, puzzles – them's my speciality.

JIM. And what about a *map* with cryptic clues on it?

SILVER. Ha! I can't think of the use for a map like that. Unless its purpose was to lead someone to a secret location.

JIM. What would *you* do if you had a map like that?

SILVER. Hide it well. And only show it to someone I trusted... with my life.

JIM. Long John Silver... are you... a pirate?

SILVER. Me? A pirate? Absolutely not!

JIM. It's just that you look, dress and... well, frankly, act quite like one.

SILVER *sings. During the song they bond* – SILVER *does tricks and visual gags. Jokes* – JIM *looks into a telescope and ends up with boot polish round his eye.* SILVER *casts a rod and reels in a blow-up shark.* JIM *reels in a pair of pants that pant-less* BLUE PETER *runs on and retrieves.* JIM *gives* SILVER *a drawing he's done of the two of them.* SILVER *sticks it on the wall beside his bunk.*

SILVER. *I might look like a pirate but a pirate I'm not –*
Although I'm wearing a bandanna and my hair's in a knot –
I might have multiple piercings and a tall leather boot

And some rather unhygienic attributes
But regardless of all that, and how I appear
I promise I'm no pirate nor a buccaneer.

BLACK DOG *and* BLUE PETER. *He says he's not a pirate nor a buccaneer.*

SILVER. *So… Don't judge a book by its cover,*
Or make assumptions before you're sure
Things aren't necessarily how they seem
So don't be premature.

I might look for adventure on the high seas
I might wear my shirt unbuttoned if I please
My language might occasionally sound uncouth

BLACK DOG *and* BLUE PETER. *He might say 'Aarghh' a lot in truth*

SILVER. *And I might be one-legged and also one-eyed*
But a pirate, I am telling you, I'm not inside.

BLACK DOG *and* BLUE PETER. *A pirate, he is telling you, he's not inside.*

SILVER. *So… Don't judge a book by its cover*
Before you know what it's like inside
Cos you could make a big assumption
That might not be justified.

I just like the image of a pirate I do
It's such a cool look, don't you think so too?
So my whole wardrobe is accessorised
With a load of sparkly bling that I've plagiarised
From every dandy pirate with a bad-ass look
Except that big show-off Captain Hook.

BLUE PETER. *Except that big show-off Captain Hook.*

SILVER. *So… Don't judge a book by its cover*
You might easily cause upset
And push away a friendship
And live with the regret.

Don't judge a book by its cover
Cos I think that you're the best

And you'll discover you can trust me, Jim
When you put me to the test.

JIM *is enthralled by* SILVER, *who now leaves him alone on deck.*

Scene Ten

The Awful Discovery

JIM. How long until we reach the island, Captain Birdseye?

BIRDSEYE (*off*). Only a couple of days now, Jim lad.

JIM suddenly steps on a rat and picks it up.

JIM. Eugh! Gross. Hang on, I've got an idea.

He runs into SILVER*'s empty cabin.*

Where shall I put it? Ha-ha! He's going to freak out.

ALEXA (*entering*). Playing 'Le Freak (Freak Out)'.

'Le Freak (Freak Out)' by Chic plays.

JIM. Alexa, stop!

The music stops.

Where's Long John Silver?

ALEXA. Do you require silver long johns?

JIM. No!

ALEXA. Purchasing reflective underwear.

JIM. Oh God, I think I hear him coming. Just get out.

He throws ALEXA *out of the porthole.* JIM *climbs into an apple barrel.*

I'm gonna burst out on him. It'll be just like how we first met except the other way around! What a barrel of laughs, eh?!

SILVER *and* BLACK DOG *enter.*

SILVER. This way, into my cabin. And you, Blue Peter. Where's he gone?

BLUE PETER (*off*). Give me a minute.

BLUE PETER *enters.*

SILVER. What are you wearing now?

BLUE PETER. French Connection. Or, as I call it: Connection.

SILVER. Now speak your mind, swabs! What's your grumble!?

BLACK DOG. Seems like someone's lost sight of our purpose.

SILVER. And who might that someone be?

BLACK DOG (*pointing to picture of* JIM *and* SILVER *hung up*). I'd say you an' the lad's gettin' a bit tight.

SILVER. Would you now? And how do you think he's going to show me the map if that's not the case?

BLACK DOG. How do you even know he's got the map?

He throws his cigarette into the barrel. There's a hiss and slight squeal from JIM.

BLUE PETER. Yeah, how do we know we're not chasing a wild goose?

SILVER. Oh, he's got the map all right. I done the sums.

BLUE PETER. Lest you put two and two together and came up with four.

BLACK DOG. Two and two *is* four, you howlin' bampot.

SILVER. Mark my words, I'll have it teased out of him soon enough.

BLACK DOG. I say we put a knife to his throat and be done with the supposing.

SILVER. No! We do it my way or no way at all.

BLACK DOG. We'd better see some results soon, Silver. Cos I heard talk of another who's after the treasure.

SILVER. Who?

BLACK DOG. The Raven.

SILVER. The Raven doesn't exist. He's a myth, a spook story
that pirates tell their kids at night. Now listen up and listen
good! Flint's treasure is in our grasp. And on my life, if you
rein in your damn hankering, you'll get your rewards.

BLUE PETER. Split three ways?

SILVER. Like I've always said.

BLUE PETER. And the boy? If he points the finger, there's a
chance we'll swing.

BLACK DOG. I say we feed him to the fish!

SILVER. You say a lot of things, Black Dog. And most of 'em
are best left unsaid. Let's just say the boy might find himself
spending a bit more time on the island than he expected.

BLUE PETER. And the captain?

SILVER. We'll deal with Birdseye on the return journey. Now,
let's get out of here before we raise any interest.

They exit. JIM *emerges from the barrel. His world has caved
in.*

JIM. Why would he do that? Why? He asked me to trust him.
And I did. To hell with you, Long John Silver! You're just a
pirate. Always will be! What an idiot I've been! And now
I'm stuck on this cursed ship with a crew of mutineers whose
only ambition is to plunder treasure – that might not even
exist! Damn you, Long John Silver. And damn this stupid
journey!!

*He rips apart his drawing and scatters it into the sea.
Thunder and lightning strike in response.*

Scene Eleven

A Storm

BLUE PETER (*entering*). A storm! I see crazy horses on the horizon.

SILVER. There's a white squall heading towards us, lads!

BIRDSEYE. Batten down the hatches! Here we go!

Physical routine involving props flying about and a leak which sprays the audience. BIRDSEYE *remains calm throughout.*

JIM. Watery hands the size of mountains coming for us.

SILVER. I ain't never seen troughs like this.

JIM. Maybe we deserve it!

SILVER. Eh?

BIRDSEYE. How I love to fight a storm!

BLUE PETER. Looks like it's winning!

BIRDSEYE. That's what makes it so thrilling!

BLUE PETER. Seems like the ocean wants to eat us alive.

JIM. Maybe we deserve to be eaten!

SILVER. What?

BLUE PETER. We've sprung a leak.

BIRDSEYE *sings.*

BIRDSEYE. *Thou shall have a fishy*
On a little dishy
Thou shall have a fishy
When the boat comes in.

Dance to your daddy
Sing to your mammy
Dance to your daddy
To hear mammy sing.

The storm subsides and an eerie calm follows. SILVER *is bewildered.*

Scene Twelve

Calm After the Storm

SILVER. Like it never was here. Still as a dead man's heart.

BIRDSEYE. Well, that was refreshing.

SILVER. Captain. What's going on?

BIRDSEYE. I can give you my expert's opinion: I'd say there's no wind. And no wind means no sailing. What are our losses, first mate?

BLUE PETER. Most of our supplies gone and three riggers overboard.

SILVER. What about the boy? Where's the boy?

BIRDSEYE. Safe. Resting up in my cabin. Fish finger?

SILVER. No.

BIRDSEYE. More for me then.

(*Sings on exit.*) *Thou shalt have a fishy*
On a little dishy,
Thou shalt have a fishy,
When the boat comes in.

SILVER. That guy is so weird! So, we lost three men overboard?

BLUE PETER. Yes.

SILVER. Tell me their names?

BLUE PETER. Okay, bit odd this – pirate names and all that. So, one of them was called Who, another was called What, and finally, there was I Don't Know.

SILVER. What the hell are you talking about?

BLUE PETER. Who went first, What went second and I Don't Know was third.

SILVER. I need names!

BLUE PETER. I've just told you.

SILVER. What have you told me?

BLUE PETER. That I know Who went over first, What went over second and third was I Don't Know.

SILVER. Okay, fine. So, you know the names of the first two?

BLUE PETER. Yes.

SILVER. So tell me their names.

BLUE PETER. I just have!

SILVER. Listen. I put you on roll-call duty, right?

BLUE PETER. Right.

SILVER. And your duty is to keep track of the crew.

BLUE PETER. Right.

SILVER. So. Who went overboard?

BLUE PETER. Correct, he went first.

SILVER. Who?

BLUE PETER. Exactly.

SILVER. What?

BLUE PETER. No, he went second. Who accidentally pulled him off.

SILVER. I've no idea. Why are you asking me?

BLUE PETER. I'm not. I'm telling you!

SILVER. You're telling me nothing apart from the fact that you know the names of the first two but not the name of the third.

BLUE PETER. I do know the name of the third.

SILVER. So what is it?

BLUE PETER. I Don't Know.

SILVER. Are you on drugs?

BLUE PETER. No. Are you?

SILVER *pulls out a gun.*

SILVER. Look. Someone's gonna get their head blown off in a minute! Tell me the name of the first rigger to go.

BLUE PETER. Who.

SILVER. The first rigger to go.

BLUE PETER. Who.

SILVER. The first rigger to go!

BLUE PETER. Who.

SILVER. Oh my God! Who fell in the sea first!?

BLUE PETER. Yes.

SILVER. Okay. Wait. Listen to me! Forget the first rigger, who went over second?

BLUE PETER. No, he went first.

SILVER. Who went first?

BLUE PETER. Correct.

SILVER. Good. What?

BLUE PETER. No, he went second.

SILVER. Which rigger are we talking about now?

BLUE PETER. Which rigger do you want to talk about now?

SILVER. I don't know?!

BLUE PETER. Okay, he went third.

SILVER. Who went third?

BLUE PETER. No, he went first.

SILVER. What?

BLUE PETER. Second.

SILVER. Right. When you enlisted the rigger that went over first, how did he sign his name?

BLUE PETER. Who.

SILVER. The rigger that went over first!

BLUE PETER. That's how he signs it.

SILVER. Who?

BLUE PETER. Yes.

SILVER *holds the gun to* BLUE PETER*'s head.*

SILVER. Final chance. If I'd been standing there watching three men go overboard, who would be the first man I'd see fall into the sea?

BLUE PETER. Correct.

SILVER. And his name is what?

BLUE PETER. No. What's the name of the second rigger?

SILVER. I don't know?!

BLUE PETER. No. He's the third rigger!

SILVER. But you don't know his name?

BLUE PETER. You literally just said it.

SILVER. And what did I say?

BLUE PETER. I Don't Know.

SILVER. I've had enough of this! Just tell me this: is there anyone left to do the rigging?

BLUE PETER. Yes.

SILVER. Tell me his name?

BLUE PETER. Why.

SILVER. Because I'm your superior and I need to know!!

BLACK DOG *enters.*

BLACK DOG. I've just been conversing with the remaining rigger.

SILVER. Why?

BLACK DOG. Yes.

SILVER. Who's the remaining rigger?

BLACK DOG. No, he went overboard.

BLUE PETER. That's what I've been telling him.

SILVER. So we've lost all four riggers now?

BLACK DOG. No, just three.

SILVER. What?

BLACK DOG. Yes, him too, but can anyone confirm the third?

BLUE PETER. I Don't Know.

BLACK DOG. Excellent. Shall I carve their names into the mast as a memorial in the order they died, Silver?

SILVER. Fine. Who was first?

BLACK DOG. Okay. And second?

SILVER. What?

BLACK DOG. Very well. And third?

SILVER. I don't know.

BLUE PETER. He's got it!

BLACK DOG. None of this changes our plan, right?

SILVER. Losing a few men? Why should it? Both of you, get out of here.

BLUE PETER *and* BLACK DOG *exit.* JIM *appears on the upper deck.*

Jim lad! I'm so relieved. I was so worried for you.

JIM. Is that so?

SILVER. We lost three souls in the storm.

JIM. Really? Who? What were their names?

SILVER. I'm not getting into all that again! The main thing is, you're safe.

JIM. And why exactly would it matter if I had been lost?

SILVER. What are you talking about? Come down 'ere, I need to speak to you.

JIM. What about?

SILVER. Is something bothering you, lad?

BLACK DOG *pokes his head through a porthole.*

BLACK DOG. What's going on? It's still as calm as a millpond out there. It's like we're cursed.

SILVER. Get out.

JIM. Why would we be cursed? Only untrustworthy double-crossing pirates fall victim to curses. And there is none of *them* on board, is there… Long John Silver?

SILVER. Course not. Wind'll pick up.

JIM. 'Day after day, day after day,
We stuck, nor breath nor motion;
As idle as a painted ship
Upon a painted ocean.'

BLACK DOG. Even the fish aren't biting now. You've brought us bad luck. We're going to die out here. And all because –

SILVER. I told you, we're not cursed! Get in there.

He bundles BLACK DOG *off.* JIM *is left alone looking out to sea.*

Scene Thirteen

A Mermaid

JIM. Maybe I should confide in Captain Birdseye – tell him everything. Tell him I lied about the voyage. But he might want to turn back. And what kind of adventure would that be? If those pirates want that map it'll be over my dead body. I'll memorise it and then destroy it and then… what? Oh, I can't do this alone. I want my mum and dad. Or… someone…

A MERMAID *appears in the sea, washing herself and singing to the tune of 'Lovin' You' by Minnie Ripperton.*

MERMAID. *Lovin' me is easy cos I'm beautiful,
Makin' love to me is all you want to do.*

La la la la la,
La la la la la,
La la la la la,
La la la laa,
Doo du du du doooo…

JIM. It's… a mermaid!? An actual mermaid! She's… beautiful. Okay, play it cool, Jim, deep breath, just look back and smile.

At that moment, the MERMAID *in harpooned by* BLACK DOG. *She sings the famous high note in pain before being dragged onto the ship. She flops around on the deck making dolphin noises.* BLACK DOG *produces a knife.*

No! What are you doing? Let her go!

BLACK DOG. Get away with you. I'm starving!

JIM. You can't eat her! She's not a fish.

BLACK DOG. You can pan-fry the bottom half.

JIM. Pan-fry her and you'll have to pan-fry me first! And if you pan-fry me, I'll pan-fry you –

SILVER *enters.*

SILVER. It's all right, Jim, no one's getting pan-fried.

BLACK DOG. We'll grill her then!

SILVER. Or grilled, baked, steamed or –

BLACK DOG. Spit-roasted?

SILVER. Especially not that! Mermaids are daughters of the sea. She possesses powers stronger than any man: she can bring us the wind! If she makes the wind blow, I'll let her go.

JIM. You promise?

SILVER. I promise. (*To the* MERMAID.) Do you understand me?

She makes dolphin noises and flaps around.

Call to the wind: make it blow!

The MERMAID *shakes her head and turns away.* JIM *looks into her eyes.*

JIM. Just do it! Please. If you do it, he'll let you go.

The MERMAID *calls out to the wind and it begins to blow.*

SILVER. Bingo! Now, Mucky Mike? Where is he? Go and wake Captain Birdseye and tell him to bring the ship about. Well, go on then! You know your way about the ship – it's been two months now.

Audience member comes up on stage and exits behind the set, through the ship.

JIM. So. Are you going to be honourable?

SILVER. Course. But just a small caveat. Thing is, Jim – she's the only thing that can secure the wind in our sails.

JIM. So?

SILVER. So it's best she stays with us until we reach our destination.

JIM. But that wasn't the deal!

SILVER. Jim, I'm doing this for you. Black Dog!

SILVER *and* BLACK DOG *shackle the* MERMAID *to the mast. She's left alone.*

Scene Fourteen

Saving the Mermaid

MERMAID. How could I have been so stupid – coming to the surface like that? My parents warned me to stay where I belong.

Mucky Mike is returning to his seat. He's now fully kitted out as a pirate.

Oh, hello. Who are you?

MUCKY MIKE. Mucky Mike.

MERMAID. Mucky Mike, unshackle me and set me free. Please!

She convinces him to help. But BLACK DOG *enters with a length of wood as a weapon.*

BLACK DOG. What are you doing, Mucky Mike? Get back below deck with the other crew. Now!

Mucky Mike exits back to his seat.

Great. A night spent chucking water over a chained-up mermaid. (*Throws a cup of water over her.*)

JIM *appears.*

JIM. I can take over if you want?

BLACK DOG. Get out of here, kid. You think I'm stupid?!

JIM. No. Quite the opposite in fact.

BLACK DOG. What's your game?

JIM. Tell me, what would you do if I attempted to release the mermaid?

BLACK DOG. Bash ya skull in with this bit of four-by-two. (*To Mucky Mike.*) You were very lucky, Mucky Mike.

JIM. What about someone your size though? I'll bet you this shiny gold coin that you can't knock yourself out with that bit of wood.

BLACK DOG. Ha, ha, ha. You're about to lose your money, kid.

JIM. Well, I guess we'll see.

BLACK DOG *knocks himself clean out.*

MERMAID. Typical man.

JIM. You can speak English?

MERMAID. Of course. And Spanish, French, Portuguese, Whales.

JIM. You mean Welsh?

MERMAID. No, Whales.

She makes a whale call. A whale responds.

JIM. Wow.

MERMAID. Are you going to release me?

JIM. Yes. Of course.

He unties the knots.

It's just that... I don't want to see you go.

MERMAID. Why not?

JIM. Because... sorry, we've only just met.

MERMAID. Don't apologise. This is the bravest thing anyone's ever done for me.

JIM. I'm not brave. If I was brave I would ask if I could...

MERMAID. Kiss me?

JIM. No!

MERMAID. No?

JIM. I mean yes. Oh God, I've landed myself into such a crazy situation on this ship. And then slap bang in the middle of all that I meet someone as lovely as you.

MERMAID. Seems like we're both young adventurers, keen to discover what's beyond the horizon.

JIM. A scared fourteen-year-old who's way out of his depth?

MERMAID. A young man who's prepared to stand up for what he believes in...

BLACK DOG *murmurs. The* MERMAID *hits him over the head with the wood.*

JIM. I don't even know your name...

MERMAID. It's A a a a a e e e e o o o w.

JIM. A a a a a e e e e o o o w?

MERMAID. No, A a a a e e e o o o o w.

JIM. A e e e e o o o w w?

MERMAID. No, that is my sister's name. What's yours?

JIM. Jim.

MERMAID. Jhem?

JIM. No, Ja–

MERMAID. Ja–

JIM. –im.

MERMAID. –im.

JIM. Jim.

MERMAID. Jhem.

JIM. That's close enough.

MERMAID. So, are you the cabin boy, Jhem?

JIM. Yes. But this is my ship, you see – I won her in a bet. And I have a treasure map.

MERMAID. That's so exciting!

JIM. But the crew are about to embark on a mutiny and steal it.

MERMAID. That's so scary. I wish I could help.

JIM. I don't think anyone can... unless...

MERMAID. Yes?

JIM. I have this 'friend' who's always wondered if there was any way that a man and a mermaid could ever be together.

MERMAID. If they kiss in the light of the full moon at midnight on the spring tide, they can be properly united.

JIM. You mean she'd grow legs?

MERMAID. Or he'd surrender himself to the ocean and become a merman.

JIM. Oh. Wouldn't it be better if...?

MERMAID. If she grew legs!? What century are you living in, Jhem? Why on earth should *she* have to make the sacrifice? It's amazing under the sea – we live in coral palaces, we have octopus servants.

JIM. So, it really is just like I imagined.

They lean in for a kiss.

SILVER (*off*). Jim!?

JIM. Quick. We need to get you back in the ocean.

He tries to lift her but they fall in a heap on the deck.

MERMAID. Just drag me.

JIM. Okay.

He drags her to the edge. She lowers herself into the water.

MERMAID. I believe in you, Jhem. Complete your adventure.

JIM. I will. Thank you. I'm going to stand up to Long John Silver and I'm going to Treasure Island.

MERMAID. Treasure Island?

JIM. Yes, do you know it?

MERMAID. It's only a short sail from here. But it's also known as… Skeleton Island.

JIM. That doesn't sound very tropical.

SILVER (*off*). Jim!?

MERMAID. Just before I go, can I clarify that your 'friend' is actually you and the 'mermaid' is me.

JIM. Yes.

MERMAID. Until we next meet.

JIM. Until we next meet.

MERMAID. Goodbye, Jhem.

JIM. Goodbye, A a a a a e e e o o o o w.

She disappears beneath the waves.

(*To himself.*) I think I love you!

SILVER *enters*. BLACK DOG *regains consciousness*.

SILVER. Oh dear, Jim. What *have* you done?

BLACK DOG. You tricked me, you scrotting sack-head!

SILVER. No. Leave this to me. Go and sort yourself out.

BLACK DOG *exits*.

JIM. I'm not a... whatever he said! I'm an adventurer and I stand up for what I believe in! The treasure is rightfully mine, to share as I see fit. And you're either my ship's cook, and then you were treated handsome, or you're just a common mutineer and pirate, and then you can go hang!

SILVER. So what's your next move?

JIM. I hadn't really thought that far ahead.

SILVER. Oh you silly little boy.

JIM. Yeah? Well, what's *your* next move? Cos you can't do much without the map.

SILVER. Well now, that's where the tables have somewhat turned for you.

He produces the treasure map from his coat.

Very well hidden. I was most impressed.

JIM. Okay, listen. Let's just talk about this.

BLACK DOG *enters with a wooden plank over his shoulder.*

BLACK DOG. Too late. He walks the plank. Unless, of course, you've grown too attached to the swab, Long John Silver?

SILVER. I don't grow attached to no one.

BLACK DOG *places the plank.*

BLACK DOG. Start walking.

JIM. Long John Silver? Captain Birdseye!

BLACK DOG. Oh, he won't hear you. He'll be tucked up in bed now.

SILVER *aims a musket at* JIM.

SILVER. Walk!

JIM *walks. He reaches the end. There's a shot. Blackout. Splash as* JIM *hits the water.*

End of Act One.

Interval.

ACT TWO

Scene Fifteen

Saving Jim

Gunshot and splash as before. Curtains open and within a huge frame (like a fish tank) we see JIM *sinking amongst bubbles (he's stood on a box with false legs). He struggles and then loses the fight to breathe. UV fish approach.* [*NB. This scene can be edited/made topical as required. Voices are best pre-recorded onto a backing track.*]

FISH 1. Oh no! A human has fallen into the sea.

FISH 2. Looks like he's having trouble breathing.

FISH 1. Mmm. That's because humans can't breathe underwater like we can.

FISH 2. Don't humans have gills?

FISH 1. No, they have lungs. And lungs don't work underwater – as we are now witnessing.

FISH 2. So we need to get him out?

FISH 1. Yes, but we'd need arms to do that.

FISH 2. I know someone who has arms.

FISH 1. Who?

FISH 2. Jenny Jellyfish.

A UV JELLYFISH *enters.*

Jenny Jellyfish? Can you help us get this human up to the surface?

JELLYFISH. No. My tentacles are all wobbly and stingy. Also, I have no brain.

FISH 1. And you poop through your mouth.

JELLYFISH. Rude.

A UV STARFISH *enters.*

FISH 2. A starfish has strong arms. Hey, Sally Starfish, can you help us save this human?

STARFISH. I'm afraid not. I only have traction on the seabed – by using the hundreds of tube feet on the underside of my body.

FISH 2. You do look pretty though.

STARFISH. I'm so pretty.

A PLASTIC BAG *enters.*

FISH 2. Hey, a plastic bag.

PLASTIC BAG. I'm not just any plastic bag. I'm a Marks and Spencer plastic bag.

FISH 2. Can you help us?

PLASTIC BAG. No, I'm afraid not, I'm being chased.

FISH 1. Who by?

A cut-out of GRETA THUNBERG *in a diving suit enters.*

GRETA. By me! Greta. You will not escape.

FISH 1. Greta, can you help us save this man?

GRETA. No. I'm too busy tackling real-world problems.

FISH 2. But we're facing a crisis.

GRETA. Indeed we are.

MERMAID (*off*). Jhem! Jhem!

FISH 2. Oh my God, it's…

ALL. A mermaid!

MERMAID *enters* (*on stilts with a false tail*). *She grabs* JIM *and gives him the kiss of life. An initially serene underwater scene* (*using all four actors*) *starts to fall apart and break down.* MERMAID *stumbles and knocks* JIM *off the box he's stood on, the frame starts to collapse. Chaos. Curtains close.*

Scene Sixteen

Arrival at the Island

SILVER *and* BLACK DOG *appear in front of the curtain.*
SILVER *is holding the map and looking out.*

SILVER. There it is, Black Dog. Treasure Island. Is *The Little Todger* prepared?

BLACK DOG. All set starboard.

There is a small rowing boat nearby.

SILVER. Flint's treasure is finally in reach.

BLACK DOG. Then let's be having it!

SILVER. Wait, what are you doing?

BLACK DOG. Getting in the boat. What does it look like?

SILVER. No, no, no. You're not coming.

BLACK DOG. What?

SILVER. I need you here to safeguard the ship.

BLACK DOG. From who?

SILVER. People like us – bad-ass pirates. Plus, I don't trust that Captain Birdseye won't leave us here stranded. All I require is someone to row me ashore. And I know just the man.

BLACK DOG. Not Mucky Mike!?

SILVER. Where is he?

BLACK DOG. The man's a total liability. He's not to be trusted.

SILVER. Oh, I think I can handle him. Get up here, Mucky Mike. Back to your position, Black Dog.

BLACK DOG. I'll be waiting.

BLACK DOG *exits. Mucky Mike gets up on stage.*

SILVER. Right, Mucky Mike, in you get. And when I say 'in you get', I mean put the boat over your head and the straps

over your shoulders. Hurry up, man. Now, take these oars
and stick them in the rowlocks. I said *rowlocks*. Good. Now,
row! Where are you going? Over there towards the island!
Hold on, we're hitting rough water – and when the boats a-
rockin'...

*They row. Improvise with Mucky Mike until the sounds of the
island seep in. Tropical but also eerie and sludgy.*

SILVER. Blimey, look at the place. You'd hardly advertise it as
paradise, would you? All right, Mike, out we get. Now,
watch my *Little Todger* until I return. And don't fall asleep or
else it's curtains for you.

Mucky Mike heads back to his seat.

What a foul belching cesspit of a place this be. Now...
Treasure I up!

He exits. Transition to...

Scene Seventeen

Ben Gunn's Place

This side of the island is more lush. JIM *lies washed up on the
beach.* BEN GUNN *appears and sings...*

BEN GUNN. *My name's Ben Gunn and I live on this isle,*
  But I haven't seen another soul for quite some while,
  So, each day I amuse myself in any way I can,
  And today could not be better, cos today I've got a man.
  Yee-haa!

Shall we have some fun?

He fills JIM's *hand with shaving foam, then tickles his cheek
and hides.* JIM *sits up and slaps the foam all over his face.*

JIM. Hello, who's there?

BEN GUNN (*off*). Hello, who's there?

JIM. Where am I?

BEN GUNN (*off*). Are you?

JIM. My name's Jim Hawkins.

BEN GUNN. Neither is mine.

BEN GUNN *appears*.

JIM. Blimey! Who are you?

BEN GUNN. Jim Hawkins.

JIM. No. I'm Jim Hawkins.

BEN GUNN. The man seems very confused.

JIM. Okay, let's start again. My name is Jim. What is your name?

BEN GUNN. 1742.

JIM. Okay. And when were you born?

BEN GUNN. Ben Gunn.

JIM. There we go. And where am I, Ben Gunn?

BEN GUNN. Skeleton Island. Just in time for afternoon tea.

He wheels in a tea trolley.

JIM. Skeleton Island? This is it. She must have brought me here.

BEN GUNN. And will *she* be joining us? What's her name?

JIM. A a a a o o o e e w.

BEN GUNN. What is she, a bird?

JIM. A mermaid.

BEN GUNN. The man's a fruitcake.

JIM. What are you doing here, Ben Gunn? How did you get here?

BEN GUNN. Nobody remembers. Not even my wife.

JIM. You have a wife?

BEN GUNN. Yip!

JIM. Is she here too?

BEN GUNN. Oh yes. And my boy. He's a son-of-a-Gunn.
Wanna meet 'em?

JIM. Yes. That'd be...

BEN GUNN. Christopher!

A monkey appears.

JIM. Whoa!

BEN GUNN. Christopher, Jim Hawkins. Jim Hawkins, my son,
Christopher.

JIM. Right. Not quite what I was expecting.

BEN GUNN. What were you expecting?

JIM. Less hair?

BEN GUNN. Christopher, go and tell your mother we have a
guest.

CHRISTOPHER *exits.*

JIM. Were you perhaps marooned here, Ben Gunn?

BEN GUNN. Marooned? Marooned? Yes, I was marooned!
Macaron?

He produces a plate of 'macarons'.

JIM. What's this made from?

BEN GUNN. Icing sugar, egg whites, ground almonds, double
cream.

JIM. It looks like mud.

BEN GUN. It is. Got any cheese?

JIM. Cheese?

BEN GUNN. Please? Ah, Louise!

CHRISTOPHER *enters operating a coconut puppet that is wearing a grass skirt.*

JIM. She's got coconuts for knees!

BEN GUNN *does her voice, Marilyn Monroe-esque.*

LOUISE. So lovely to meet you, Jim.

She adjusts her coconuts.

JIM. Lovely to meet you too... Louise.

LOUISE. Thanks. Have a seat. Shall I pour?

She swings her arm at the teapot. It just clanks about.

JIM. Perhaps I can help you?

Louise sits on JIM*'s lap and strokes his head.*

LOUISE. Thank you. Proper gentleman. Real tidy manners.

BEN GUNN. Louise!

She jumps off.

JIM (*pouring*). Well, it's certainly been a while since I've had a lovely hot cup of... sand?

BEN GUNN. And what brings you here, Jim? You must be on some kind of adventure.

JIM. Well, the truth is... I had a map, you see.

BEN GUNN. What kinda map? With clues?

JIM. Yes.

BEN GUNN. What kinda clues? Cryptic?

JIM. Yes.

BEN GUNN. A treasure map?

Louise starts to shake.

Calm down, Louise, or you'll fall apart again! Show me the map.

JIM. I can't. It was stolen from me, along with my ship, by a pirate called Long John Silver.

BEN GUNN. Left leg cut off at the knee, eye patch, a parrot called Alexa!?

JIM. Yes.

BEN GUNN. Nope, never heard of him. But what I can tell you is that this island is layered with the souls of a hundred failed treasure-seekers, whose only comfort is to live an eternity of insect-ridden hell! Are you sure you don't have any cheese on you?

JIM. Quite sure.

LOUISE. More tea?

JIM. I'm still enjoying this one thanks.

Louise strokes her (washing-up glove) hand down his body to his crotch.

LOUISE. Strawberry cheesecake? Lemon meringue pie? Knickerbocker Glory?

BEN GUNN. Christopher, take your mother off for a lie-down! She's had quite enough stimulation for one day.

CHRISTOPHER *exits with puppet.*

Thanks for playing along.

JIM. Sorry?

BEN GUNN. I know that the tea's sand, my son's a trained monkey and my wife's made outta coconuts.

JIM. It must get very lonely here.

BEN GUNN. Ben Gunn has to find out who he's dealing with, you see. Especially now that Jim Hawkins' ship's arrived.

JIM. My ship?

BEN GUNN. Yip. Out there.

JIM. They're here!

BEN GUNN. A man with a log for a leg already arrived on the other side of the island.

He picks up The Little Todger.

The guard had fallen asleep. Unfortunate for him – (*Looks at Mucky Mike.*) Yip! Boat best kept in the care of Ben Gunn.

JIM. Oh my God, Ben Gunn. Who *are* you?

BEN GUNN. Tickety tick, tickety tick, the race is on, Jim must be quick.

JIM. Wait. You must know this island like the back of your hand.

BEN GUNN. Every path, every turn, every tree, every slope, and what I can't reach, through my telescope!

JIM. So we could find the treasure together and share it. We could get back to my ship and –

The sound of distant gunshots. Both look out. JIM *takes the telescope.*

Another tender leaving *The Jolly Todger*?

BEN GUNN. Ben Gunn'll track that boat. Yip. If Jim finds himself in a bit of a fix, then blow on this shell, I'll be there in two ticks. Seek out your treasure, boy. (*Hands* JIM *a bag with a large seashell in it.*)

JIM. *Our* treasure, Ben Gunn.

BEN GUNN. And watch out for the acid bogs on the north side of the island.

JIM. Acid bogs?!

BEN GUNN. Eat a man alive in seconds. Go!

JIM exits.

Christopher?

CHRISTOPHER *enters.*

The Raven. I can sense him. We must get to work!

Scene Eighteen

The Raven

SILVER *enters. He shoots three scary offstage animals* (*sound effects only*) *– a rattlesnake, a vulture, a wild boar – and then a fourth – a sheep. He refers to the treasure map.*

SILVER. The final clue. I'm so close, I can smell it. (*Reads.*) Below the yellow fingers, two steps of a civilian, and six feet below, ten thousand million. Yellow fingers?

ALEXA *enters.*

ALEXA. Contacting fellow swingers.

SILVER. No! Where's Flint's damn treasure!

ALEXA. Getting directions to Flint's treasure.

SILVER. Really? What direction?

ALEXA. Searching for songs by One Direction.

SILVER. No! I'm gonna throttle you in a minute, you scrawny wretch! Switch to security mode. Go and keep a lookout. Below the yellow fingers? (*Sees a banana tree.*) The bananas! It means the banana tree. And two steps beyond – (*Takes two steps.*) six feet below… it's under my feet. Get digging, Long John Silver. Get digging!

Music transition to move time forward until SILVER*'s spade hits something solid.*

The years I've spent searching for this vessel! And finally, it's mine. All of this lovely… (*Opens the chest.*) sand!? What in hell's kitchen is this!? I've been had!!

ALEXA. Security alert. Intruder detected.

SILVER. Alexa, get here. Hide!

He grabs ALEXA *and hides.* JIM *enters.*

JIM. The three ribbed steps – it must be these – and then the final clue, what was it? Come on, Jim, think. Something about yellow fingers… ah ha! Bananas! That banana tree. And… oh my God.

He sees the open chest and rushes over to it, picking up a big handful of sand.

Sand?

SILVER. Well, well. Look who's crawled out of the sea.

JIM. Long John Silver. What's going on?

SILVER. I think that's a question for you... Jim lad.

He points the musket at JIM.

Where's the real map?

JIM. There! In your hand.

SILVER. This one? That's led me to a chest full of sand!? You've swapped them.

JIM. I haven't.

SILVER. You're lying!

JIM. I never lie!

SILVER *clicks the safety catch off.*

SILVER. Where's the real map, Jim?

JIM. I no more fear you than I fear a fly, Long John Silver. Kill me, if you please, or spare me.

SILVER *is about to shoot when* BIRDSEYE *enters.*

BIRDSEYE. Hello, gents. Having fun?

SILVER. Oh great. Now Santa's turned up. Birdseye, get back to the ship, this doesn't concern you.

BIRDSEYE. Oh, it does a bit. Blue Peter?

BLUE PETER *enters, aiming a musket.*

SILVER. Blue Peter, what are you doing? Put that gun down.

BIRDSEYE. I should save your breath. He's no longer the man you knew.

BLUE PETER. *Thou shalt have a poisson on a little croissant, Thou shalt have a poisson when the boat comes in.*

Dance to your mama,
Dance to your papa,
Dance to your mama,
To hear mammy sing.

SILVER. What's happened to you, man? Pull yourself together!

BIRDSEYE. I've told you, you're wasting your time. I've reprogrammed his brain.

SILVER. You've done what?

JIM. He's been brainwashed.

BIRDSEYE. Oh, it's a little more sophisticated than that, isn't it, Blue Peter?

BLUE PETER. Oui oui, Maman.

SILVER. What? Who *are* you?

BIRDSEYE. You see, it was just as obvious to *me* as it was to *you* back in old Blighty, that this – (JIM.) scamp here had the map. Bobbing up in that barrel was a nice move, by the way. Capture his imagination by playing the wild eccentric, eh? But I think you'll agree, it was an even neater trick to let him 'win' my ship and then for you to organise a crew to sail me here to Skeleton Island.

He swaps into a top hat to become POSH BLOKE, *from before.*

POSH BLOKE. 'What say you put your inn up against... Oh, I don't know. One of my ships? That one.'

JIM. You're the one Billy Bones warned me of. You're...

SILVER. The Raven!

In horror, SILVER *tries to shoot himself. But* BIRDSEYE *pulls a pistol and blows it out of his hand.*

BIRDSEYE. Don't do that, Silver. Not yet, at least. Tie them up, Blue Peter.

BLUE PETER *ties them to a tree.*

So, if this map has led to a chest of sand – (*Rips it up.*)
where's the real one?

SILVER. He's hidden it.

JIM. That's the map I took from Billy Bones' trunk! That's all I
know.

SILVER. He's lying.

JIM. Why would I lie? I don't even care about the treasure any
more. Maybe *you're* lying. Maybe you've already found the
treasure and have hidden it somewhere else.

SILVER. Why would I do that?

JIM. Well, let me think. Because you're a dirty, double-crossing
pirate.

BIRDSEYE. Oh dear. What a spot of bother you both present
me with. Blue Peter, I think we'd better show them what
happens to those who cross the Raven, don't you?

BLUE PETER. Oui oui, Maman.

BLUE PETER *strings up a back-projection screen* (*large
white sheet*). BIRDSEYE *puts on an apron.*

BIRDSEYE. Now then, we're going to magic up some of
Captain Birdseye's famous fish fingers, loved by children
and adults alike. Now who can eat the most fish fingers in
one sitting? (*Impro with audience.*)

BLUE PETER. All ready, Maman.

BIRDSEYE. Would you like to see my famous fish-finger
machine in action, boys and girls? Let's turn the lights on then.

A back-projection light reveals (*in shadow*) *a fearful-looking
contraption.*

But before we begin, we just need to oil the cogs. So, have
you got your oil can, Blue Peter?

BLUE PETER. Oui oui!

He reaches inside (*in shadow*).

BIRDSEYE. Now, can you see the blades?

BLUE PETER. Oui, c'est magnifique, Maman.

BIRDSEYE. Good. Then let's get fish-fingering!

BIRDSEYE *uses a remote control to fire the machine to life.*
It's loud, it's grinding, BLUE PETER *is sucked in. Blood*
(ribbon) spurts out of the top and fish fingers drop onto a
silver platter. BIRDSEYE *sings (slightly demonic)...*

I delight to serve up
At teatime
The scrummiest, scrummiest, scrummiest, scrummiest
Scrummiest food I'm able.

Because I know that you deserve
Only the best,
Only the best, only the best,
The best for the captain's table!!

BIRDSEYE *presents his platter to the secured* SILVER *and*
JIM.

Go on, try one. Mmmm. Simply irresistible. Golden crispy
every time. You can't get your fingers on finer fillets. No? Oh
well, more for me. You have until sunset to get your story
straight, or else it'll be the captain's table for you both.

He exits, singing.

Scene Nineteen

The Plan

JIM. Oh. My. God.

SILVER. Well, this lands us in a bit of a pickle.

JIM. A bit of a pickle!? Unless we come up with a solution
we'll be turned into goujons.

SILVER. Fish fingers.

JIM. They're the same thing! If only I could get to that shell in my bag.

SILVER. Some scallion's got here before us.

JIM. How? How would they discover that chest *without* the map!?

SILVER. So explain that chest full of sand.

JIM. I don't know! Just let me think!

Pause.

I would have shared the treasure with you – the idea of that didn't even cross your mind, did it? Why are adults so greedy!?

SILVER. What's done can't be undone. Right now, the path to outwitting the Raven begins with us working as one.

JIM. Except I wouldn't trust you further than I can spit at you!

SILVER. Harsh.

JIM. You made me walk the plank. And then you shot me!

SILVER. *At* you. I missed. And Long John Silver never misses, eh.

JIM. And I'm supposed to be *thankful* for that!?

SILVER. Well, you survived, didn't you? How *did* you survive, actually?

JIM. You don't have an ounce of moral decency about you.

SILVER. Listen. I'm a pirate. That's what pirates do. And I didn't choose to be like this neither. I was brought up on the wrong side of the tracks.

JIM. Oh please! So are lots of people. But that doesn't give them the right to act like utter tosspots!

SILVER. Okay. I'm sorry, all right. And for what it's worth... I think you're a kid in a million. If you were my son –

JIM. But I'm not, am I?! I'm not your son and you're not my dad! And you never will be!

SILVER. No. I will say this though. You have the pirate within you.

JIM. You could *not* be more mistaken.

SILVER. Really? Then how did old Blind Pew meet his maker, eh? And more to the point, your aunt?

JIM. How do you know about that?

SILVER. Old Silver just done the sums.

JIM. It was an accident. It was all an accident.

SILVER. Think of it: your experience till now. With you, smart as paint. An adventurer for life. You'd rule the seas.

JIM. And live by thieving and dodging the rope at every turn?

SILVER. Exactly. The romance of it. Tempting, innit.

JIM (*struggling*). Not in the least.

SILVER. Talking of romance… you and that mermaid.

JIM. It's none of your business!?

SILVER. I'm just saying, if you want any advice.

JIM. I don't.

Pause.

SILVER. I went bareback horse-riding with a mermaid once.

JIM. No you didn't!

SILVER. Listen, we don't have time for this. We must think as one!

JIM. Think for yourself!

SILVER. Aarghh! God, this is *so* embarrassing. Tied with my back to a mast, I'd accept – there's respect in that, a yarn to tell. But sat on me arse under a flipping banana tree? Very disrespectful to a man of my calibre. By the way – why did you want that shell?

JIM. Will you *please* shut up? I'm trying to think!

SILVER. Yeah well so am I!

Passing time. SILVER *falls asleep.*

(*In sleep.*) Ten thousand million…

JIM. Ten thousand million what? Stars? Sand? Wait… grains of sand. Of course! I've got it! Wake up.

SILVER. What?

JIM. Ten thousand million… grains of sand. It's simply *part* of the clues. Just like in Billy Bones' trunk, there must be a map hidden in the lining. I'm sure of it.

SILVER. Being sure of it is all very well. But how are we going to find out?

JIM. Alexa.

SILVER. Alexa!?

She flies in.

JIM. Fly to the chest and look behind the lining.

ALEXA. Playing 'Hi Ho Silver Lining'.

'Hi Ho Silver Lining' by Jeff Beck plays.

SILVER *and* JIM. No!!

The music stops.

SILVER. Open the chest and look in the lid.

ALEXA *flies to the chest, rips at the lining and discovers…
a map.*

JIM. She's got it!

SILVER. Thank the heavens for that. Now bring it to me.

ALEXA. Did you say 'drop in sea'?

SILVER *and* JIM. No!

SILVER. Alexa, heel!

ALEXA *lands on* SILVER*'s shoulder with the map in her
mouth.*

Right. We give the Raven the map and be done with it.

JIM. And you think he'll just let us go!?

SILVER. Have you got a better plan?

JIM. Yes I have. Now listen.

They confer in hushed whispers as BIRDSEYE *approaches.*

BIRDSEYE. *Thou shalt have a fishy*
On a little dishy
Thou shalt have a fishy
When the boat comes in.

My goodness, that last batch tasted good. Well?

JIM. We have the map.

BIRDSEYE. Oh. I'm glad you've come to your senses. Show me.

SILVER. Go ahead, Alexa. 'Cept it needs deciphering. Cos this lad, you see, smart as paint, rewrote it with his own messaging.

ALEXA *delivers the map to* BIRDSEYE.

JIM. So we'll need to accompany you. Show you the way.

BIRDSEYE. Very well. But if you try to cross me, you'll be yummy yummy in my tummy.

He unties SILVER *and points a musket at him.*

Now untie him.

SILVER *starts to untie* JIM. *His body hides* JIM *from view, then he stands.*

SILVER. Although.

JIM. What are you doing? Untie me. Like we agreed.

BIRDSEYE. What's going on?

SILVER. The boy is not to be trusted.

JIM. What?!

SILVER. He took me into his confidence to explain his coding to me, but unfortunately for him, that's now rendered him... expendable. And since I know him to be nothing but trouble...

He kicks JIM *in the face and knocks him out.*

We should leave him here for the vultures. I alone will lead you to the treasure.

BIRDSEYE. Very well, pirate. On your life *alone* be it. Walk.

SILVER. This way.

They exit.

Scene Twenty

All Seems Lost

We are left with JIM. *Motionless, with* BEN GUNN's *shell now at his side.* JIM *comes to.*

JIM. Well, knocking me out *for real* wasn't part of the plan. Okay, here we go. Oh man, if blowing on this shell fails, we're both dead.

He manoeuvres his body until he is able to blow on the shell. In an instant, BEN GUNN *appears.*

BEN GUNN. What's up? You found some cheese?

JIM. Ben Gunn! Thank goodness.

BEN GUNN. Might the lad be in a spot-of-a-bother?

JIM. Wait, how did you get here so quickly?

BEN GUNN *runs fast on the spot.*

BEN GUNN. Ben Gunn reeeaaaally likes to run.

JIM. Have you been following me?

BEN GUNN. Nope.

JIM. Have you?

BEN GUNN. Nope.

JIM. You have, haven't you.

BEN GUNN. Yip! But not in a creepy way. Just checkin' up. You're lookin' mighty tied to that banana tree there.

JIM. Yes, well, if you wouldn't mind…

BEN GUNN. My pleasure. Been a while since I've had the opportunity to untie a man. Or tie one up for that matter.

He unties JIM.

JIM. Thank you. And now I really do need your help. There's a man. Captain Birdseye.

BEN GUNN. I know.

JIM. But he's not what he seems.

BEN GUNN. I know.

JIM. He's the most feared individual that walks the earth.

BEN GUNN. They call him the Raven.

JIM. I know.

BEN GUNN. The nightmare of every living pirate.

JIM. I know.

BEN GUNN. And he seeks Flint's treasure.

JIM. Wait, how do you know what I know?

BEN GUNN. Same way you knows what I knows.

JIM. Right, I need you to come clean with me. How did you come to be on this island?

BEN GUNN. You sure you don't have any cheese?

JIM. What is this cheese obsession!?

BEN GUNN. Monterey Jack's my favourite by a country mile.

JIM. Listen. If you help me, I'll get you a slab of Monterey Jack as big as a house! What happened to you?

BEN GUNN. Cabin boy. Same as you. Smart as paint.

JIM. And who left you marooned in this godforsaken place? Pirates?

BEN GUNN. Friends. My friends: Captain Flint, Billy Bones, Blind Man Pew... Ben Gunn trusted them all with his life. He was just a boy with nothing but hope in his heart. But they were grown men with nothing but greed in theirs. You gotta stand up to 'em.

JIM. I intend to. I have a plan. But I need your knowledge of the island.

BEN GUNN. Like I told ya, Ben Gunn knows the old Skeleton Isle better than the isle knows itself.

JIM. That's what I'm counting on.

BEN GUNN. Ben Gunn and Jim Hawkins are fruits of the same tree. Pears, apples, bananas. We're like a fruit salad.

JIM. You're certainly that. Come on.

BEN GUNN. Not that way. This way.

JIM. But they went that way.

BEN GUNN. Easy to lose your footing in the dark on that path.

JIM. But it's still light.

BEN GUNN. Night falls quickly on the island.

JIM. Yeah, but surely not that quickly.

Suddenly we're plunged into darkness.

JIM. I stand corrected.

BEN GUNN. Follow me!

Scene Twenty-One

Putting the Plan into Action

It's dark and creepy. SILVER *enters, followed by* BIRDSEYE *pointing a gun.*

SILVER. So if I am not mistaken – this be the north side of the island.

BIRDSEYE. My patience is wearing thin, Silver! Fourteen clues and we appear to be going around in circles.

SILVER. Have faith, Captain Birds– Actually, how should I address you now? The Raven? Captain Ravens-Eye?

BIRDSEYE. I'm beginning to think of putting an end to you and going back for the boy.

SILVER. No! That won't be a necessary course of action, I can assure you. Just let me...

(*Reads*.) 'On your left you will find
A coconut tree, note the plumbing...'

That must be the tree. And the plumbing to note must be... this root?

'Step and discover
Your next clue is coming.'

Okay.

He steps on the root. A musical whoosh. A human skull swings in.

Aarghh! Jesus.

There's a scroll in the eye socket, which he removes.

I have to say, a lot of work has gone into setting all this up. I mean, it takes a lot of thought.

BIRDSEYE. Are you going to keep yapping, little doggy, or am I going to have to render you permanently quiet?

SILVER. I'll stick to the clues...

(*Reads*.) 'Don't let the ground below you
Fill you with dread,

But know it by name,
It's the home of the dead.'

Seems fitting that death and treasure be in one bed.

BIRDSEYE. With one more soon to be joining its ranks unless he hurries.

SILVER. There's more.

(*Reads*.) 'The stone that respects it
Shall mark the spot
When an ample moon tilts through
Its eye in the top.'

There, that must be it! And the beam through the hole points… there! Here's the place to dig!

He digs and hits something hard. He reaches in and pulls out… a plug.

A plug?

BIRDSEYE. What!!?

SILVER. Wait, there's an inscription on the back.

(*Reads*.) 'The spigot you have pulled,
You should know plugs the route,
Through which every trapped soul,
When released will then shoot.'

SILVER *looks down into the hole.*

Well there doesn't seem to be… .

From the hole, a jet of a hundred trapped souls is released.

'Stand your ground, seekers,
You're about to be wealthy
Your final coordinates
Will be shown by the kelpie.'

Laser lights spin about in the smoke until they create an 'X'.

There! Up on the other side of the gorge. 'X' marks the spot. It's the end of the rainbow!

BIRDSEYE. Then get to it, Silver, and start digging. Where are you? Silver!?

SILVER (*off*). I've spent the last three years searching for Flint's treasure. Long John Silver doesn't give up without a fight.

BIRDSEYE. Then show yourself and we'll fight to the death.

SILVER (*off*). While two more make off with the prize?

BIRDSEYE. What two? There's no one left. The whole crew are fish fingers.

SILVER (*off*). Except the two digging.

JIM *and* BEN GUNN *appear on top of the hill, digging.*

BIRDSEYE. How in damnation? Who *are* they!?

SILVER. Two cabin boys. Jim Hawkins and the marooned Ben Gunn.

BIRDSEYE. How have you done this!? I'll rip them apart.

He lurches in their direction but is suddenly caught in sinking mud, hissing and gurgling.

What's going on!? I can't... my feet... they're burning.

SILVER. If Jim's idea has gone to plan, I believe you're standing in what's known as an acid bog.

BIRDSEYE. Help me, I'm sinking!

SILVER. Lie down, spread your weight, you'll dissolve quicker.

BIRDSEYE. Silver! We can come to an arrangement. You'll need protection. The treasure will be the death of you.

SILVER. No. I think it's going to be the death of *you*.

BIRDSEYE. I'll haunt you in your dreams, Silver!

And he's gone. But suddenly, BIRDSEYE's *skeleton shoots back up out of the mud – but it's just a final death throes.*

SILVER. Dead men don't bite, Monsieur Fish Finger!

Scene Twenty-Two

Finding the Treasure

SILVER *calls up to* JIM *and* BEN GUNN.

SILVER. Jim Hawkins. Ben Gunn. He's crossed his luck and spoiled his Bible for the last time. How do I reach you?

JIM. You don't.

SILVER. What!?

JIM. The tender is waiting in the bay below to take me and Ben to *The Jolly Todger*. The treasure will return with us to England and you, Long John Silver, will be left to rule Skeleton Island in any way you see fit, and out of harm's way for the rest of us. Just as your plan had been for me.

SILVER. You scalliant fuddy mucker, you double-crossing, pant-wetting rogue! You're only safe because of me. You swore to me you had principles, Jim Hawkins, you will rot in hell for such treachery.

JIM. Silver! Silver! Calm down, will you, you great timber-legged fool. I'm joking.

SILVER. What!?

JIM. I'm pulling your leg.

BEN GUNN. Well, his remaining one.

SILVER. Hilarious. I'm going to kill both of you.

JIM. Throw him the rope, Ben Gunn.

> BEN GUNN *throws him a long rope*.

> Swing yourself across the acid bog.

SILVER. Yeah, right. And then you slice the rope when I'm halfway across. I wasn't born yesterday, kid.

JIM. Long John Silver, have I ever lied to you?

BEN GUNN. Have you?

JIM. No. Have I?

SILVER. I suppose not.

JIM. And I'm not going to start now that I'm grown up.

BEN GUNN. Aren't you?

JIM. No. Do you trust me?

BEN GUNN. Should he?

JIM. Yes.

SILVER. I've never trusted anyone.

JIM. Well, maybe now's the time to start.

BEN GUNN. Is it?

JIM (*to* BEN GUNN). Will you shut up?!

SILVER. Very well, Jim Hawkins. I trust you.

> SILVER *'swings' himself across and lands safely on the other side.*

JIM. Long John Silver, Ben Gunn. Ben Gunn, Long John Silver.

BEN GUNN. I've heard a lot about you.

SILVER. I heard you were dead.

BEN GUNN. Nope. Got any cheese?

JIM. Will you please stop with the cheese.

SILVER. Actually I have got a Babybel.

BEN GUNN. Woooo-wee!

> *He snatches it from* SILVER *and puts it straight in his mouth.*

JIM. No, Ben, wait, you've got to take the wax off it first!

> BEN GUNN *starts choking and spitting it out.*

BEN GUNN. Ben Gunn's not sure he likes cheese no more. You got any weed?

JIM. Will you just focus!?

BEN GUNN. Split three ways, right?

SILVER. Of course. Give me the spade.

JIM. Split three ways, right, Long John Silver?

SILVER. You have my word! Here. (*Hands* JIM *his gun.*) Now
let's get digging.

*He digs. He hits something solid. The three of them raise the
chest.*

This is it.

JIM. This is it.

BEN GUNN. This is it.

They slowly open the lid.

Well, would you look at that…

SILVER. In the name of all that is holy! Where's the stonking
haul?

SILVER has retrieved a scroll. JIM *takes it and reads.*

JIM. 'Congratulations, ye courageous,
    Who have made it to the end.
    To make it thus far with your life
    Is a feat I must commend.
    Those to weather such a storm
    Are far between and few.
    What ye hold now in your hands
    Is the treasure you pursue.'

SILVER. What is this horse manure?!

JIM. 'The treasure is the journey,
    The adventure, the great endeavour.
    The friendships struck, the battles won,
    The memories that'll last forever.
    The treasure is, and will always be,
    A feeling in your heart.
    And this nugget that I pass to you,
    To others you must impart.'

BEN GUNN. That is a beautiful sentiment.

SILVER. It's the most almighty load of snowflakey woke drivel I've ever heard! Where's the treasure!?

JIM. It was only ever a message?

BEN GUNN. Well, if that ain't real treasure, I don't know what is.

SILVER. Shut up, shut up! SHUT! UP!! That can't be it?!

SILVER *starts digging deeper with his hands.*

I have not travelled halfway across the world to hear some vomit-inducing platitude telling me to be a good friend. I am not leaving this island until I have what I came here for! Where is it!?

BEN GUNN. I'd keep your voice down, you'll anger the island.

SILVER. What?! Anger the island!? Anger the island!?

BEN GUNN. Exactly.

SILVER. Gold! Gems! Diamonds, pearls, rubies, emeralds! They've gotta be here somewhere!

There's a deep rumbling.

JIM. What's going on, Ben Gunn?

BEN GUNN. Yip, he's angered the island.

JIM. What do you mean?

BEN GUNN. The volcano.

JIM. What volcano?

BEN GUNN. I call her Suzy. She wants to put on one hell of a show for us. I'd advise heading to your ship before it's too late.

SILVER. Where's the treasure?!

JIM. There is none! We have to get off this island right away. Come on.

JIM *drags* SILVER *by the arm, but stops and turns around. The volcano erupts.*

Ben, what're you waiting for? Come on!

BEN GUNN. No, no. I'm staying right here. This is where I belong.

JIM. But you'll be –

BEN GUNN. Trust me, Jim, I'll be fine. And here – a little souvenir for you! But promise you won't eat 'em till you're home. Hurry!

JIM *catches the coconuts* BEN GUNN *throws.* JIM *and* SILVER *run. The sound of the volcano erupting transitions into waves against the ship.*

Scene Twenty-Three

The Journey Home

JIM *stares into the waves.*

SILVER. Come on, Jim lad, it's been seven nights now since the full moon rose on the spring tide. And not a single sign of her.

JIM. I know she'll come.

SILVER. Okay. But look, there's something I need to tell you. How do I put this…? You see, love between a man and a woman is a wonderful thing and… but with a mermaid things aren't quite so… simple. You see, there's this thing called desire…

JIM. Long John Silver. Are you trying to tell me facts of life? Seriously? I'm nearly fifteen! I've killed people!

SILVER. I'm just trying to help!

JIM. Listen, wanting to see her again is not about wanting to be together. I know that's not possible.

SILVER. Oh right.

JIM. Becoming a merman is not the life for me and I wouldn't expect her to... you know.

SILVER. Live in a tank above your bed?

JIM. Become fully human! I just want to thank her. And say goodbye. Because without her, I wouldn't be standing here right now.

SILVER. You're a good lad, Jim lad.

SILVER exits. Piano intro begins.

JIM. Where are you? All I want to do is see your beautiful face again. Where are you?

JIM starts to sing a version of 'Total Eclipse of the Heart' by Bonnie Tyler. The MERMAID appears behind JIM –

MERMAID. *Turn around.*

– but he is too lost in his song to notice her at first, even when she resorts to hurling plastic sea-life at him and keeps singing 'Turn around.' When the song reaches the line 'And I need you now tonight', JIM finally turns to see the MERMAID, and they move towards each other to embrace. SILVER takes over the vocals. A giant squid dances seductively in the background but goes too far with a pole dance. The lyrics at the end of the song are adjusted to –

JIM *and* MERMAID. *Once upon a time we were falling in love But now we know we must live apart There's nothing we can do It's like a total eclipse of the heart.*

The MERMAID jumps away backwards, waving, but trips and falls into the wings.

Scene Twenty-Four

Losing *The Jolly Todger*

SILVER *steps out*.

SILVER. Jim. I would've…

JIM. Would've what?

SILVER. Made the same decision, of course. Your paths will cross again one day.

JIM. Maybe.

SILVER. Just like yours and mine.

JIM. Not on the high seas, Long John Silver.

SILVER. Once a treasure-hunter, always a treasure-hunter.

JIM. Not me.

SILVER. Come on, lad. The people I could introduce you to: the infamous Anne Bonny, Mary Read. Pirates with more cunning and strength than any man I know. What a team we'd make.

JIM. And I'm telling you, it's not the life for me.

SILVER. Well. The offer was there. (*To himself*.) Right, Plan B. (*Back to* JIM.) Until we reach Blighty, we'll at least eat like pirates.

JIM. With what? We have no provisions left. Well, except those coconuts, but I promised Ben Gunn I wouldn't open them until I got home.

SILVER. By the morning we'll reach the coast of Ireland. You take that gold coin of yours – do you still have it…?

JIM. Yes.

SILVER (*to himself*). I was counting on that. (*Back to* JIM.) And you buy us as many potatoes and leeks as it'll stretch to – to go with these plastic fish.

He exits.

JIM (*to audience*). And what a mistake that was.

Cut to: he's standing in a marketplace.

STALLHOLDER. Top of the mornin' to you there, sir. What can I do you for?

JIM. As many leeks and potatoes as this coin will stretch to, please.

STALLHOLDER. Ah, you're planning a broth then? Bit of a MasterChef, are we?

JIM. No. But my ship's cook is.

STALLHOLDER. You own a ship, do ya? I'll bet you have the craic scooting around in that thing.

JIM. It's been quite an adventure already.

STALLHOLDER. Out there in the bay, is she?

JIM. Yes – the three-masted schooner.

STALLHOLDER. The one that's sailing off into the open water with a pirate flag being hoisted?

JIM. What? No! No! Long John Silver, you absolute –

Ship's honk.

– you steaming pile of –

Ship's honk.

– you can take that ship and shove it up –

Ship's honk.

– arse!

SILVER. Sorry, Jim lad, it's in my bones. Once a pirate, always a pirate. I have to find that treasure. It's gotta be out there somewhere. Oh, here, don't forget your souvenirs.

He throws the netted coconuts to JIM.

And that was the mistake *he* made. I just didn't know it yet. Until I'd been home a week.

Scene Twenty-Five

Home

JIM *prepares the bar. A* POLICEMAN *is reading back through his notes.*

POLICEMAN. So let me get this straight, Mr Hawkins. Accounting for your six-month absence, you say... you went on holiday.

JIM. Well, that was the original idea.

POLICEMAN. After you found a treasure map in your dead lodger's belongings.

JIM. Yes.

POLICEMAN. And then you claim to have won a ship in a game show, sailed to the Caribbean, been saved from drowning by a beautiful mermaid who left you on an island full of skeletons where you met a crazy old man who lived with a coconut wife and a monkey son, who helped you escape the clutches of a cannibalistic fish-finger tycoon.

JIM. Nasty piece of work.

POLICEMAN. You then had to quickly depart from the island because it was about to blow up but on your way home, your ship was stolen from you by a one-legged pirate.

JIM. Basically yes.

POLICEMAN. How old are you?

JIM. Fourteen.

POLICEMAN. You sound like a bit of a dreamer to me, son.

JIM. You're not the first person to say that.

POLICEMAN. But back to the purpose of my visit – the circumstances of your aunt's death? Did you notice anything suspicious before you left? And please... keep it simple!

JIM. No.

POLICEMAN. Right, thank you, Mr Hawkins. I'll be in touch
   if I need anything else. But I think I'll leave your rather
   creative tale out of my report.

JIM. Thank you, officer.

   He exits. A PUB CUSTOMER *has been watching from the
   bar, quite drunk.*

PUB CUSTOMER. You know what, Jim? This story of yours.
   It'd make a remarkable work of fiction.

JIM. But it was all true.

PUB CUSTOMER. Course it was. Another one of these, please.

   JIM *heads behind the bar.*

   Actually, scratch that. All this talk of the Caribbean has got
   me in the mood for… a piña colada!

JIM. A what?

PUB CUSTOMER. White rum.

JIM. Got that.

PUB CUSTOMER. Pineapple juice.

JIM. Think we've got a tin of that.

PUB CUSTOMER. And coconut cream.

JIM. Ah, I'm afraid I haven't got any co– hang on a minute. Yes
   I have!

PUB CUSTOMER. Fantastic. Just going for a wizz.

   He walks into a post.

   Sorry, madame.

JIM. It's that way.

   He exits. JIM *produces a coconut.*

   But how on earth do you get into a coconut?

   *He cracks it down on the bar. Jewels spill out. He grabs the
   other one. The same.*

The treasure... Ben Gunn, you son of a gun!

Split focus with BEN GUNN *back on the island, with a chest of gold, singing.*

BEN GUNN. *My name's Ben Gunn*
I'm a son of a gun,
I tricked everyone
Yeah that's what I done,
Cos I buried all the loot
Then re-hid it, how astute
And then designed a new route
And all the cryptic clues to suit.

But it's not what you might think
This isn't for my pleasure,
I didn't hide it for myself
I'm just warden of the treasure.

Cos it's best kept away
From those who seek great wealth
Cos mainly they stay greedy
And divide us from good health.

JIM. I'd like to say that I went back to thank Ben Gunn. But oxen and wain-ropes would not bring me back again to that accursed island. So, I used the treasure to refurbish the inn and now, just like in my dad's day, and in memory of both my parents – The Admiral Benbow is once again a place where everybody knows your name.

He sits at the harpsichord and sings 'Where Everybody Knows Your Name'. The POLICEMAN, PUB CUSTOMER *and* VANESSA *from the game show enter as customers and join him.*

The End.

[NB. In the original production, 'In the Navy' by Village People was a curtain-call song, with BIRDSEYE *at the ship's wheel and the other cast members singing and dancing in hot pants.]*

www.nickhernbooks.co.uk

facebook.com/nickhernbooks

twitter.com/nickhernbooks